Sustainable Land Use Initiatives in Mizoram

Sustainable Land Use Initiatives in Mizoram

A Study of New Land Use Policy

James L.T. Thanga

SHIPRA

ISBN: 978-93-86262-04-2

First Published in India in 2016

Sustainable Land Use Initiatives in Mizoram: A Study of New Land Use Policy

Published by:
SHIPRA PUBLICATIONS
LG 18-19, Pankaj Central Market
I.P. Ext., Patparganj, Delhi 110092, India
Tel.: +91 11 2223 5152/6152
E-mail: info@shiprapublication.com
www.shiprapublication.com

ACKNOWLEDGEMENTS

It is a great pleasure for me to complete this book which required vigorous effort and collection of a wide variety of information from personal records, office documents, and research papers. At the very outset, I deeply acknowledge the support given by the NLUP Implementing Board (NIB), Government of Mizoram. Indeed, the study attempts to generate reliable analysis without any political bias, meaning that the failure of the state government would have to be highlighted in some areas. In spite of this, the government, especially the Chief Minister Mr. Lal Thanhawla himself, showed great zeal in such kind of research work. This should be applauded by the academic community. It would be an impossible task to try and present credible analytical information without the openness of the government in accepting the reality, which may not be in their favour in some of the cases.

During the pursuit of data collection and analysis, I received constant support from various officials of NLUP Implementing Board, Government of Mizoram. I owe deep gratitude to the Chairman Mr. J.H. Rothuama, the Vice Chairman Mr. P.L. Thanga, and Secretary Mr. James Lalrinchhana for their enthusiasm and support for the preparation of this book. I am also indebted to Ms. Sophie Lalnunpuii, Technical Officer of NIB, who was always ready to furnish the required data. I am deeply appreciative of Prof. Thangchungnunga and Dr. Laltanpuii Ralte for readily sharing their documents and research papers.

It is my privilege to thank my close friend Mr. Lalthanchhunga for his encouragement and moral support throughout the research period. I also extend my heartfelt thanks to my colleague Dr. Lianhmingthanga for all his help and painstakingly proofreading the entire manuscript. I am immensely grateful to my wife, H. Rosangpuii, for being a constant source of love and encouragement.

Lastly, as said earlier, this book attempts to present reliable information without having inclination to any particular ministry under a political party. I do, however, accept that this book is not without errors. And if any part of the book hurt or upset the readers, I express my sincerest apologies in advance.

CONTENTS

LIST OF ABBREVIATIONS

ACA	–	Additional Central Assistance
AH & Vety	–	Animal Husbandry and Veterinary
ALSC	–	Agriculture Land Settlement Certificate
APEDA	–	Agriculture Products Export Development Agency
APR	–	Actual Payee Receipt
BDO	–	Block Development Officer
BNRGSK	–	Bharat Nirman Rajiv Gandhi Sewa Kendra
BRGF	–	Backward Region Grant Fund
CBO	–	Community Based Organisation
CCEA	–	Cabinet Committee on Economic Affairs
CEDAR	–	Centre for Ecology Development and Research
CFPF	–	Captive Farming on Passion Fruit
CSS	–	Centrally Sponsored Scheme
CYMA	–	Central Young Mizo Association
DC	–	Deputy Commissioner
DL and S	–	Department of Land Revenue and Settlement
DLMC	–	District Level Monitoring Committee
DPR	–	Detailed Project Report
EO	–	Extension Officer
FAO	–	Food and Agriculture Organisation
FFS	–	Farmers' Field School
Ha	–	Hectares
IFAD	–	International Fund for Agricultural Development
ILO	–	International Labour Organisation
INC	–	Indian National Congress
ISOPOM	–	Integrated Scheme of Oilseeds, Pulses, Oil Palm, and Maize

ITC – Integrated Training Centre
IWMP – Integrated Watershed Management Programme
JCP – Jhum Control Project
LAD – Local Administration Department
LSC – Land Settlement Certificate
MGNREGA – Mahatma Gandhi National Rural Employment Guarantee Act
MIFCO – Mizoram Food and Allied Industries Corporation Ltd.
MIP – Mizoram Intodelhna Project
MIRSAC – Mizoram Remote Sensing Application Centre
MiSALT – Mizoram Slope Agriculture Land Technology
MNF – Mizo National Front
MNRE – Ministry of New and Renewable Energy
MoU – Memorandum of Understanding
MPC – Mizoram People Conference
MT – Metric Tonnes
MTA – Mid-Term Assessment
NABARD – National Bank for Agriculture and Rural Development
NABCONS – NABARD Consultancy Services Ltd
NBM – National Bamboo Mission
NCA – Normal Central Assistance
NEC – North Eastern Council
NFDB – National Fisheries Development Board
NIB – NLUP Implementing Board
NLUP – New Land Use Policy
NMMP – National Mission on Medicinal Plants
NOC – No Objection Certificate
NSS – National Sample Survey
OM – Operation and Maintenance
PPP – Public-Private Partnership
PC – People Conference
PRRS – Porcine Reproductive Respiratory Syndrome
RD – Rural Development
RKVY – Rashtriya Krishi Vikas Yojana
S & WC – Soil and Water Conservation
SHG – Self Help Group
SLMC – State Level Monitoring Committee
S & ME – Small and Micro-Enterprises

SME	–	Special Micro-Enterprises
SPAB	–	State Purchase Advisory Board
TM	–	Technology Mission
UD & PA	–	Urban Development and Poverty Alleviation
UNDP	–	United Nations Development Programme
UNIDO	–	United Nations Industrial Development Organisation
UNO	–	United Nations Organisation
UT	–	Union Territory
VC	–	Village Council
VCP	–	Village Council President
VLIC	—	Village Level Implementing Committee
VLMC	–	Village Level Monitoring Committee
VLW	–	Village Level Worker
WRC	–	Wet Rice Cultivation

LIST OF TABLES AND FIGURES

LIST OF TABLES

LIST OF FIGURES

INDIA
MIZORAM

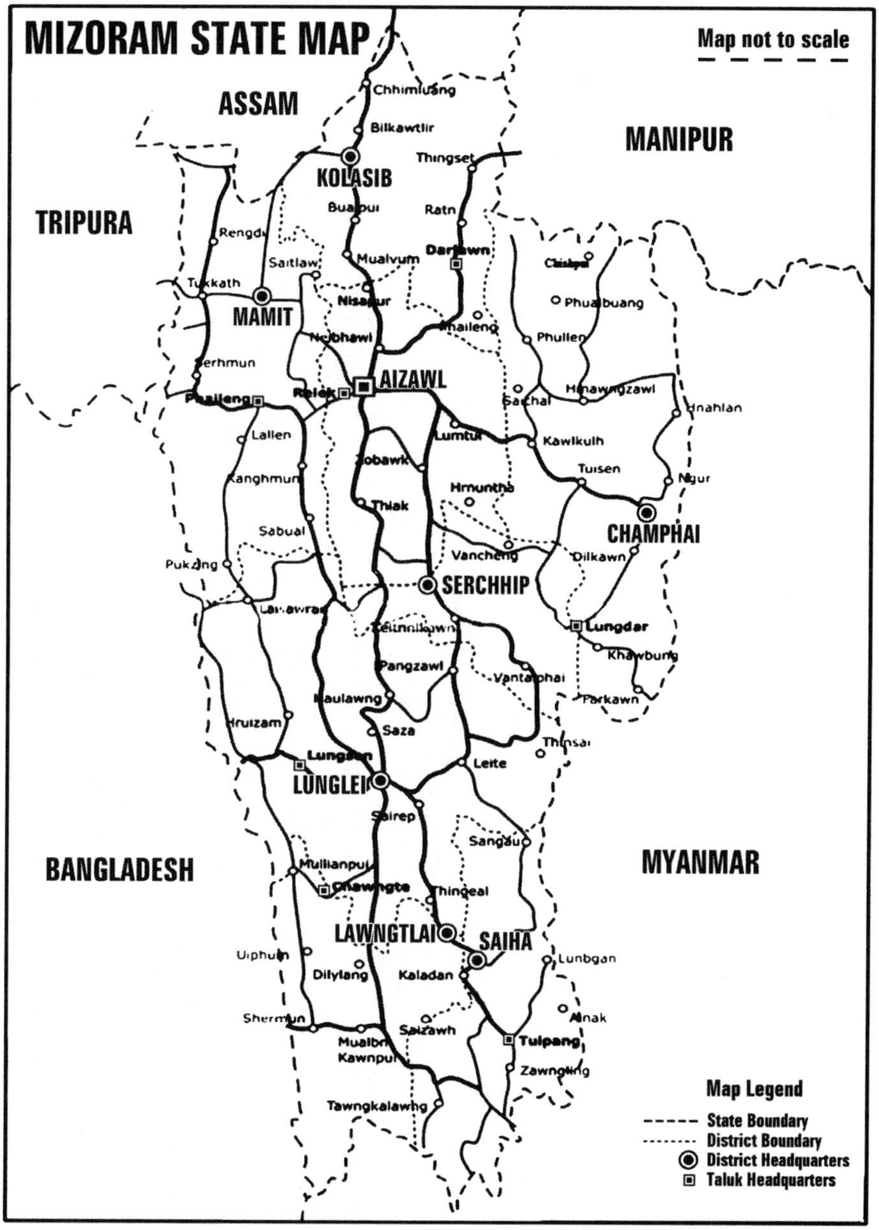
MIZORAM STATE MAP
Map not to scale
ASSAM
MANIPUR
TRIPURA
BANGLADESH
MYANMAR
Chhimluang
Bilkawtlir
KOLASIB
Thingset
Ratn
Mualvum
Saitlaw
Tukkath
MAMIT
Nisapur
Phualbuang
Phullen
Thaileng
AIZAWL
Serhmun
Lallen
Lumtui
Kawlkulh
Hnahlan
Tuisen
Ngur
Kanghmun
Zobawk
Hmuntha
Thiak
CHAMPHAI
Sabual
Vanchen
Dilkawn
Pukzing
SERCHHIP
Lungdar
Khawbung
Pangzawl
Vantaphai
Parkawn
Hruizam
Saza
Thinsai
Leite
LUNGLEI
Sairep
Sangau
Mullianpui
Chawngte
Thingeal
LAWNGTLAI
SAIHA
Lunbgan
Uiphum
Dilylang
Kaladan
Shermun
Saizawh
Ainak
Tuipang
Mualbu
Kawnpui
Zawngling
Tawngkalawng
Map Legend
State Boundary
District Boundary
District Headquarters
Taluk Headquarters

1

INTRODUCTION

The state of Mizoram, with total geographical area of 21087 sq. km, has a hilly terrain and lies in the easternmost corner of India sandwiched by Bangladesh and Tripura in the South-West, Myanmar in the East, and the Cachar district of Assam and Manipur in the North. It is divided into eight administrative districts – Mamit, Kolasib, Aizawl, Champhai, Serchhip, Lunglei, Lawngtlai, and Saiha. According to the 2011 census, the total population stood at 10,97,206 with a density of 52 persons per sq. km, and there are 830 census villages, of which 704 are inhabited. The majority of the population in Mizoram are Mizo who belong to the Mongoloid stock. Majority are Christians (87.16 per cent), and the Scheduled Tribe population constitutes 94.43 per cent. The state is amongst the most literate states in India where the literacy rate is 91.33 per cent, with male and female literacy rates respectively 93.35 per cent and 89.27 per cent. Mizoram is an agrarian state and majority of the population in rural areas practise shifting cultivation. The total area under shifting cultivation during 2010-11 was 28542 hectares with 68433 families undertaking it, which is 64.67 per cent of rural households.

The term 'shifting cultivation' as is practised in Mizoram has been defined in different ways, mostly according to the various activities undertaken in it. According to Conklin (1961), shifting cultivation is any continuing agriculture system in which impermanent clearances are cropped for a shorter period in years than they are followed. To anthropologists, it is swidden or slush-and-burn and to the Indians, it is described as jhumming, while in Mizoram, the natives called it 'tlanglo' (Thangchungnunga, 1997). In the system of field operation in Mizoram, jhum sites are shifted to a new location every year with the rotational period ordinarily varying from 5 to 10 years. The duration of this jhum cycle depends on the acreage of land available for cultivation. Different villages have different endowment of land areas, which give rise to variation in the cycle period. Shifting cultivation, in its more traditional and culturally integrated form, is an ecologically and economically viable system of agriculture as long as population densities are low and jhum cycles are long enough to maintain soil fertility. However, with changing requirements of the growing population, jhum cultivation becomes devastating in nature, causing drastic decline in crop yield, loss of forest wealth, soil fertility, biodiversity, and environmental degradation (Mishra and Saha, 2007). The need to develop alternative and sustainable form of land utilisation that can replace shifting cultivation was felt by the elites since long time back.

Historically, the Mizo were agriculturists even before they migrated from the Far East to the Lushai Hills during the 18th Century. The only form of farming known to them was shifting cultivation which formed the major activity of the Mizo economic life, and this is retained even today. Wet rice cultivation which was reported to be practised in the year 1921, by the Mizo residents of Burma (Myanmar), is the first recorded adoption of a settled form of cultivation among the ethnic groups of Mizo (Lalthangliana, 1980). Due to limited availability of flat land for farming on permanent basis, the people had the habit of carrying out shifting cultivation year after year. They remained a semi-nomadic tribe even after entering into Mizo Hills and the mode of cultivation which they followed was the most wasteful type of land use. After the lands within easy reach from the village were used up, they had to shift the village site, thus making shifting cultivation imperative (Shakespeare, 1917).

The annexation of Mizoram by the British in 1890 brought some changes in the age-old agricultural system. Firstly, Major H.W.C Cole took the first step for transformation of agricultural administration in the area by initiating rubber plantation at Chite in Aizawl during the year 1908-1909 (Ralte, 2016). Secondly, he introduced settled method of cultivation of orange, pineapple, and other fruit crops, and also of vegetables like mustard, cabbage, etc. Thirdly, he developed a vegetable demonstration farm at a place called Hmuifang. These marked the beginning of sustainable land use practices in Mizoram by the introduction of settled cultivation.

The state of agriculture experienced significant change after the establishment of Lushai Hills District Council in 1952, which was subsequently changed to Mizo District Council in 1954 under Sixth Schedule of the Indian Constitution. The District Council took the responsibility of regulation of jhumming as well as control and allotment of lands for other agricultural purposes. With the abolishment of chieftainship in 1955, all the land rights previously vested in the chiefs were transferred to the democratically elected village councils. They inherited village lands from the village chiefs and made allotment of land to the village members for cultivation within their respective village jurisdiction.

The District Council lasted till 1972 when Mizoram was elevated to Union Territory (UT) status. Though the people began to realise the adverse impact of shifting cultivation, the only significant effort shown by District Council administration was jhum regulation, and no notable initiative was undertaken for agricultural development. At the time when Mizoram was one of the districts of Assam, the Department of Agriculture made a rather insignificant beginning (Thangchungnunga, 1997). With the inception of UT in 1972, a full-fledged Directorate of Agriculture was established with a number of administrative and field staffs. This expansion in the administrative personnel was in line with the emphasis given to agricultural development in the plan outlays since the Fifth Plan (1974-79). The government started to show substantial budgetary effort for agriculture development since the beginning of the Fifth Plan by allocating sufficient share of plan expenditure to it.

Since the start of the Fifth Plan, there has been persistent attempt to abolish the practice of shifting cultivation among the rural population through gradual shift to permanent system of land utilisation. Different ministries initiated different models of land use policies from time to time. The first state-sponsored project, for the adoption of sustainable land use practice and moving of the people away from shifting cultivation, was introduced by People Conference Party Ministry under the leadership of Brig. T. Sailo. It introduced 'Garden Colony' scheme during the annual plan of 1977-78. Financial assistance to households settled under the scheme was spread over a period of five years in a phased manner. Activities adopted under this scheme were wet rice cultivation (WRC), cultivation of potato, and terracing of hill slope. The record of the Directorate of Agriculture showed that as many as 1545 beneficiaries were covered under the scheme. However, before this scheme had time to take any definite shape, it was discontinued by the new ministry that came into power in 1984.

The Congress Party that came into power under the leadership of Lal Thanhawla in 1984 initiated a land use policy by incorporating Integrated Rural Development Programme (IRDP) into a comprehensive policy, named 'New Land Use Policy (NLUP)'. The main objective of NLUP was to move the jhumia families away from their jhumming practices to settled and sustainable livelihood activities. A total of 15076 families were assisted with a total expenditure of Rs. 344.2 lakh under the scheme. However, the scheme was implemented for a period of three years only (1984-85 to 1986-87) due to change in the ministry following the signing of 'Peace Agreement' between the Mizo National Front (MNF) and the Government of India in 1986, and the upgradation of Mizoram to a full-fledged state in 1987. The new ministry of MNF under Laldenga discontinued NLUP, and introduced 'Jhum Control Policy (JCP)' on a pilot basis in selected blocks in 1987-88. However, the scheme could not make much headway due to the political setback of MNF Party in the election of 1989.

The new Congress ministry reinstalled the NLUP scheme during 1990-91, and the programme lasted till 1996-97. 49025 families from 12 RD blocks were covered under this scheme. Again, the scheme was discontinued after the Congress party lose the election in 1998. The MNF ministry that came into power under the leadership of Zoramthanga initiated a project for self-sufficiency of Mizoram, named 'Mizoram Intodelhna Project (MIP)' in 2002. However, the policy could not attain notable achievement due to a number of reasons, one of which is the political setback of MNF party in the election in 2008. The Congress party under Lal Thanhawla re-initiated the NLUP in a more comprehensive way in 2009 following its landslide victory in the Assembly Election towards the end of 2008. The scheme is more comprehensive than all the previously implemented sustainable land use policies in terms of coverage, amount of assistance, project management system, funding pattern, etc. It was launched during the financial year 2010-11 on 14 January 2011 and was set for a period of five years till 2014-15. However, the state government has decided to extend the period of the scheme upto 2018.

Mizoram has seen several initiatives to abolish the traditional practice of shifting cultivation by introducing several sustainable land use practices since the later part of the 1970s. Of these initiatives, NLUP occupies a unique place as it was implemented three times by the same party under the same leadership. Right from its inception in 1984, their coverage were sufficiently large with substantial expenditure. The central objective of all the initiatives was to abolish shifting cultivation and move the families involved in it away to sustainable system of cultivation and other livelihood activities. Although the positive impacts of these schemes could be seen in a number of cases, the practice of shifting cultivation persists in Mizoram even today. Since this is the case, it is considered necessary to study the various dimensions of these policies towards achieving their main objectives, and also the areas where they failed. This book gives a study of the several initiatives of the Government of Mizoram for the emergence of sustainable land use practices, with the case of NLUP being given more emphasis.

The analysis and observations presented in this book are expected to serve meaningful purposes. It would be a useful input for the development of land use policies in the future by learning from the successes and failures of the past. Although the state had implemented several land use policies in the past, it is difficult to get reliable data for meaningful analysis even from official records, due to frequent change of the persons dealing it. This is basically due to the loss of attention when the party that initiated the policy was replaced by another political party. Meanwhile, the people also lack the habit of keeping proper records of any activity they had undertaken. As such, one cannot say that the data currently available will be accessible in the future. Consequently, it is important to document the existing data and also make unbiased analysis so as to enable a smooth transition of the information of project-related activities to the future generation. Thus, the book is expected to fill this gap, and would be a useful source of information for further policy initiatives.

Normally, the land use policies adopted in Mizoram in the past encompassed several schemes specifically made for some activities, while they also initiated several projects to be undertaken within a specific time frame and budget. Readers of this book are informed in advance that the terms 'policy', 'schemes', and 'project' are used synonymously to denote a particular land use policy. Similarly, 'shifting cultivation' and 'jhumming' or 'jhum cultivation' are also used as synonyms in the presentation. Further, the analyses were primarily made using secondary data, and findings and observations of previous researches, while primary data was used in a limited number of cases only.

2

DYNAMICS OF LAND TENURE SYSTEM

2.1. Introduction

Land Tenure system is closely connected with the way in which natural surroundings can be exploited (Thangchungnunga, 1993). Food and Agriculture Organisation (FAO) defines land tenure system as the relationship, whether legally or customarily defined, among people, as individuals or groups, with respect to land. It is an institution, i.e. rules invented by societies to regulate behaviour, and is a system that determines who can use what resources for how long, and under what conditions. Generally, land tenure is categorised into four - private, communal, open access, and state. Private land indicates the land right assigned to a private party who may be an individual, a group of people, or corporate body such as commercial entity or non-profit organisation. Secondly, communal lands are lands where the right of common exists within the community and in which every member has the right to use the land independently. Thirdly, there are lands that are not specifically assigned to anyone and no one can be excluded, which are commonly termed 'open access' lands. Lastly, lands to which the rights for its uses are assigned to some authority in the public sector are called state lands.

From known history of the tribe, agriculture has been practised as the primary source of livelihood in Mizoram. Until 1894, when the Christian missionaries introduced elementary education, the Mizo society remained non-literate, and was without any written language. Among the Mizo people, who combined herding with hunting and agriculture, land tenure derives from the theory that all land is vested in the hands of the head of tribe or chief. Land administration in Mizoram had undergone several changes since its annexation by the British in 1890. The British Colonial regime was the first to introduce changes in land administration in 1898 when the absolute power hitherto enjoyed by the chiefs was transferred to the colonial administration headed by the Superintendent. However, village lands were apportioned to the then chiefs to be managed by them, like it used to be, without much intervention. At the same time, the chiefs were compelled to collect house tax, called *Zoram Chhiah* (residence surcharge), from all their subjects which would further be submitted to the colonial administrators. Democratic institution of land administration came with the inauguration of Lushai Hills District Council in 1952 under the Constitution of Independent India wherein the Council was given the power to enact laws relating to the allotment of land for agricultural purposes. Excepting minor amendments, Rules made by the District Council were in force even after the state was elevated to the status of Union Territory in 1971 and, its consequent up-gradation to a full-fledged state in 1987.

2.2. Land Tenure System in the Traditional Mizo Society

The land in which the tribe lived was owned by the chief in the same way that today's family property is legally owned by the head of the family (Thangchungnunga, 1993). Most lands within the jurisdiction of the Mizo were claimed by the chief as their personal possession. Within such framework of tenure, land was apportioned by a chief (who is assisted by his council) to the families according to the importance of their social position. Though the simplistic social structure of the Mizo society recognised no distinction of class, a hierarchical distinction existed on the basis of bureaucracy. Before the era of colonial rule, the value of land was expressed neither in terms of money nor any other commodity, and was never bought, sold, or traded. This is partly because there was annual rotation of jhum fields and frequent shifting of the village site itself. In such a situation, the ownership of land was not accompanied by any sense of power or prestige derived from it. It was the resources of the land which gave it value, rather than its acreage.

During the independent rule of the chiefs, a highly stratified form of society was prevalent in regard to land rights. The chief had the right to choose, before anyone else, his plot of land within the demarcated area of the jhum field. This right was exercised specially in the days when the administrative duty of the chief was rewarded with labour rather than by any other kind of tribute. Among his subjects, the chief would select a group of aristocrats, who on a priority basis were next to the chief in the selection of annual cultivation plot. There were known as *Ramhual*, and they enjoyed the right to select their jhum land every year ahead of the common people. One important qualification for the family to be nominated to this class of *Ramhual* is its capability to provide a strong work force. As they cultivated the most fertile portion of the land, they were expected to produce sufficient grain for their own consumption and for the tribute to the chief (Seletthanga, 1990).

Another privileged group was *Zalen* (Free). They were a group of landed-gentry known by that name because of their liberty to exercise pre-emptive rights in choosing jhum land. This group mostly included the elders or council members who, by virtue of their office, came into close association with the chief or were close blood relatives of the chief. Unlike the *Ramhuals,* they had to pay a paddy tribute, called *Fathang,* of the same quantity as the common people. After these privileged groups, the commoners would choose their plot of jhum land mostly according to their social positions where a relatively wealthy person had precedence over the poor and weaker citizens. Commoners could also be elevated to such privileged position by achieving the status of *Thangchhuah,* which can be attained in two ways – (i) organising social feasts and performing other rituals through storage of wealth for disposal at an occasion called *Khuangchawi*; and (ii) for those who cannot conduct *Khuangchawi,* they can achieve *Thangchhuah* position through individual abilities like hunting wild animals and their bravery in saving the people from their enemies. They were called *Pasaltha. Thangchhuah* families were given the same status as *Zalen* in land selection. The chief had no right of continuous control or detailed supervision over any land that had been granted to a family or individual and the right of enjoyment and usage of the land could not be taken way except on charges of social crimes.

In addition to these, there were established conventions which form an integral part of land relation in the village community. Their rights and claims may be enumerated as follows:

The Chief

In the pre-annexation days, the Lushai chief was regarded as the "Lord of the Soil" which, in theory, implies that he has an absolute right of division and disposal, appropriation and redistribution of land within his village boundaries. Although he enjoyed absolute right of land ownership, he was, in practice, restrained by customary observances of social justice. The right to dispose of land, for example, did not in any sense authorise him to sell, or rent, or even loan it to non-residents of the village. He had to see that every family in the village has sufficient land to work in, and so, his disposal right amounts to nothing more than monitoring the disposal of land according to individual rights. The chief, on behalf of the village community, exercised power to direct communal works of the village such as construction of aqueducts, paths, bridges, building of houses for new migrants, etc. To recompense for the administrative work of the chief, a paddy tribute (*Fathang*) had to be paid to the chief by every family of the village.

The Priest (Puithiam)

In a typical Mizo village, there were two types of priests, known as *Bawlpu* and *Sadawt*. The former was concerned with the sacrifices of the whole community while the latter served as the priest of the clan. The services of the priests were remunerated in paddy or repaid indirectly by labouring in their fields and by giving them a portion of the meat used in sacrifices.

The Village Crier (Tlangau)

In the capacity of his official position, the village crier mainly functioned as the agent of public information. Information regarding the administrative decisions taken by the council of elders or the chief that requires public notification was carried on through the crier's proclamation on the street. He is at the beck and call of the chief to announce his orders. In some villages, he may be paid a basket of paddy as remuneration for his service, and in others, a right to select the jhum land of his choice.

Blacksmith (Thirdeng)

In the traditional Mizo community, the blacksmith is a village official who works for all alike. His main duty was to provide and repair the tools and implements of the villagers. In return of his service to the community, he would receive, on an average, two days free labour in his field, or was paid a basket of rice from each house in the village after harvest (Lalchungnunga, 1990).

The Village Community as a Whole

A resident member of the village community enjoyed multiple rights that are of far-reaching significance in the analysis of communal land system. The status of communal land implies that it cannot be bought or sold but is utilised in the best interests of the community. This very concept guaranteed the individual the right to collect fallen dried timbers at all times; to cut house building materials such as posts and planks in their cultivated areas, and to pick any wild fruits. At the same time, an individual's land right could not pose any obstacle in making a passage way through any part of the village land. All the villagers had equal right to the use of paths and water-holes, the grazing land over any uncultivated area, and the right to cut thatch. Sungrass is the material used for thatch which grows scantily over the hill forests but forms a very valuable building material. Because of this, its extraction was regulated by certain codes. For instance, if anybody needs and tends a patch of thatch grass, he acquires the right to cut it first and nobody can dispute his executive right of extraction. A public declaration was made every year to announce the time for cutting the grass, and any violation of the declaration was punishable with a fine of some kind.

2.3. Institutional Change in Land Tenure System

In 1873, the British Government passed a legislation called "Inner Line Regulation" to regulate the dealings between the inhabitants of the plains and the hill tribes. Again in 1898, the British introduced delineation of village boundaries in order to simplify administration and facilitate the construction of roads. By the provision of Inner Line Regulation, outsiders were prohibited from holding lands within the line and trade across the line was also regulated. There was no regular land revenue system and a house tax, *Zoram Chhiah,* was levied by the colonial administration through the village chiefs.

With the inauguration of Lushai Hills District Council (then changed to Mizo District Council in 1954) on 25 April 1952, a democratic institution was installed in the state. Under the Sixth Schedule of the Constitution of India, the District Council has the power to make laws with respect to:

i. the allotment, occupation or use, or the setting apart of land other than any land which is a reserved forest, for the purposes of agriculture or grazing or for residential or other non-agricultural purposes or for any other purpose likely to promote the interest of the inhabitants of any village or town;
ii. the management of any forest that is not a reserved forest;
iii. the use of any canal or water course for the purpose of agriculture;
iv. the regulation of the practice of jhum or other forms of shifting cultivation;
v. the establishment of village or town committees or councils and their power;
vi. any other matters relating to village or town administration;
vii. the appointment or succession of chiefs or headmen; etc

Actual transfer of power, however, took place only after the chieftainship was abolished by the Assam Lushai Hills District (Acquisition of Chief's Right) Act, 1954. Consequently, the office of chiefs was abolished and democratically elected village councils emerged in its place. Since then, the allocation of land was made by these elected village councils through a draw of lots. A political revolution that had brought about the defeat of the institution of chieftainship also heralded the effective overthrow of landed privileges by social gradation. Every citizen now had equal chance of getting a piece of the land without being dominated, because allotment became fully based on the draw of lots.

By the Ordinance of an Act of Parliament, Mizoram was given the status of Union Territory (UT) on 20 January 1972. Consequent to this, the Mizoram Legislative Assembly came into existence on April, 1972 and the Mizo District Council dissolved and ceased to exist. However, the laws made by the District Council were to be in force until altered, repealed, or amended. Similarly, the inauguration of Mizoram to statehood on 20 February 1987 affected no laws made by the Legislative Assembly of UT. In the new formulation of the land policy, ownership is statutorily vested in the government and the government, in turn, formulate laws by which to govern different shades of ownership within the state. Jhum and forest lands are governed by the Jhumming Regulation Act of 1954 and Mizo District (Forest) Act 1955 respectively.

2.3.1. Community Land

It may be recalled that jhum lands are owned communally and the village councils are empowered to make allotment of jhum fields. No individual who belongs to the village community is debarred from getting his share of jhum plot nor is he entitled to sell or transfer it. Every member of the community has the right to use the land and he does not have to pay land revenue of any form. In every village, there is a class of land which specifically belongs to the category of community land. The ownership of land or the right of occupancy is vested on the concerned jhumias only for a period of one or two years; after which it again comes under the authority of the community or village council. This land is used for jhum cultivation on a rotational basis. The rotation period depends on the area and population of the village, which usually range from 5 to 10 years. The land that belongs to the community is divided into various types.

First, there is '*safety reserve forest*' which encircles the village with a depth of about one and a half kilometre. Even in the primitive community, the Mizo villagers kept reserved forest land adjoining the entire perimeter of the village. Accordingly, the creation of village safety reserve forest was given due recognition by the Mizo District (Forest) Act 1955. This safety reserve forest is necessary for the protection of the village from fire especially during the burning of jhum fields. It also helps to preserve the balance of ecology in the interest of the community health. Second, there is a '*village supply reserve*' owned by the District Council but controlled and managed by the Village Council. This type of forest falls under the category of '*Protected or Partially Protected forest*' and is out of bounds for agriculture. Any resident of the village may cut trees and bamboos from the supply reserve for his domestic needs. Bamboo reserve forest, called *Mauhak,* also falls into this category. The right to access the supply reserve extends to all alike without discrimination but on the condition that the person is in real need of it for domestic utility. The possibility of commercial exploration is thus forestalled in the principle of use. However, practices are different from village to village in regards of fixing the area and location of the reserved forest. Third, every village has its own *burial ground* within the vicinity of the village site which is maintained by the community. All members of the village community have equal access to it.

2.3.2. Government Land

In fact, ownership of land is vested in the government since all the lands of the chiefs became the property of the District Council through the enactment of Acquisition of Chiefs Rights (Act), 1954. But the classification of ownership is based on the enjoyment of rights to use land. In this sense, government lands are those that are exclusively possessed by the government. They may be classified into the following categories:

(a) District Council (State) Reserve Forest

Any land that the state has the authority of exclusive use and disposal constitutes a council (state) reserved forest. Exclusively owned and protected by the government, acts like felling of trees, setting fire, and clearing and breaking up of land for any purpose are prohibited in such areas. By the provision of the Mizo District (Forest) Act 1955, any part of land within the jurisdiction of the council may be declared as council reserved forest. In addition to this, all the lands within one mile on either side of the major rivers are declared to be *Riverine Reserve Forest,* and all the forests within 30 metres on either side of the major highways are *Roadside Reserve Forest.*

(b) Protected Forest

This is constituted in the interest of the village communities for the protection of forests from being destroyed by careless uprooting. Under the provision of the Forest Act, the government can declare any part of communal land to be a *protected forest area,* within which private access is restricted. Clearing of any portion of such lands or extracting any material for private use without the prior permission of the government is prohibited.

(c) Wildlife Sanctuary

It is a policy decision of the government to take over possession of some land that should be protected from encroachment or any other activity. With the increase in population, more lands are cleared every year for jhum, and forests are rapidly destroyed to such a point that rare species of wildlife are in danger of extinction. In order to make the people aware of the impending threat, the state government notified wild life sanctuaries. Table 2.1 presents the status of various categories of reserved forest in Mizoram in 2011.

Table 2.1
Areas under Various Categories of Reserved Forest in Mizoram, 2011

Sl. No.	Type of Forest	Area (in Sq. Km)
A	**State Owned Forest**	6192.08
	1. Riverine Reserved Forest	1832.50
	2. Inner Line Reserved Forest	570.00
	3. Roadside Reserved Forest	97.20
	4. Other Reserved Forest	1963.63
	5. Wildlife Protected Areas	1728.75
B	**District Council Forests**	**2562.00**
C	**Total Reserved Forest**	**8754.08**

Source: *Economic Survey 2015-16*, Department of Planning and Programme Implementation, Government of Mizoram

2.3.3. Private Land

It may sound contradictory to speak of private ownership of land because it had been noted that ownership of land is vested in the government. However, even at the time of colonial rule, the administrators from time to time allotted lands in the form of a garden pass or periodic patta to the growers of orange and cotton. A system of periodic patta had also been adopted for settled agriculture. This is because most of the land belongs either to the Government or District Council or Village Councils, and whenever an individual owns land of any form, he does so for a limited purpose. To conform to the system of land ownership in the state, '*Pattas*' and '*Garden Pass*' were mere lease documents whereby land is given on lease to the Mizo for specific purposes.

The emergence of democratic institution in 1952 and the consequent abolition of chieftainship in 1954 gave birth to a new legislative system of land rights. As per The Mizo District (Land and Revenue) Rule, 1956, the Executive Committee of Legislative Assembly is the controlling authority. The following forms of land rights were incorporated in the Rule:

(i) Rights of Pass Holder (Periodic Patta)

A pass holder has usufruct right and exclusive occupancy of the land for which a pass holder right is granted. He has no right in the soil beyond the right of a user nor does he have the right to sublet, transfer, or inherit beyond the period of the pass. On the expiry of the terms of lease, his right would also cease to exist. He is, however, allowed to relinquish his estate by obtaining a written permission from the administrator within a valid period of time. As per the Mizo District (Land and Revenue) Rules, 1971, people who possess agricultural land passes/permits can convert the same to a regular Land Settlement Certificate (LSC).

(ii) Right of Settlement (LSC) Holder

This settlement holder has heritable and transferable right of use or the right to sublet his land so long as he does not violate the terms and conditions given in the settlement certificate.

(iii) Land Settlement of Non-Tribals

No land shall be settled except on periodic lease for a non-tribal who has no permanent residential pass. But those who had been living in the Mizo District since the time of his parents and who are born and brought up in the District may be granted permanent settlement. To safeguard the interest of the native against any possible land alienation, the Mizo District (Transfer of Land) Act 1963 forbids any transfer of land to non-tribals.

In July 2013, The Mizoram (Land and Revenue) Rules, 2013 was enacted wherein it is stated that allotment of land for agricultural purposes is to be made either by period patta or by land lease for specific tenure and for specific purposes (e.g. commercial plantation, horticultural farming, etc.). When applying for a P. Patta, a No Objection Certificate (NOC) from the concerned Village Council is required. A P. Patta is valid for five years, and is renewable, and can be converted to an Agricultural Land Settlement Certificate (ALSC) with consideration of the situation of quality of land use, annual revenue payment, and validity of the patta. At the same time, the ALSC holder has absolute ownership, heritable, and transferable rights, but is required to pay land revenue every year. It may also be noted that

The Rules 2013 did not give any authority to the Village Councils in respect of land settlement, except for the issuance of NOC.

The Mizoram (Land and Revenue) Rules 2013 did not give much recognition to the Village Council, except on the management of community land. As per this Law, community land means any land or area of land recognised by the locality or its surrounding people as 'Community Land' which includes, but not limited to, village safety reserve, village supply reserve, grazing areas, water bodies, playgrounds, graveyards, and other such common-use land or area. According to Section 41, the concerned VCs have to apply to the Land Revenue and Settlement Department to demarcate the land reserved for community land. The Department makes survey, fix boundary pillars, and accordingly, declares the land as a community land by issuing a notification. This can be used for special purpose or other seasonal farming or cultivation for one year.

2.4. Transition from Jhum to Settled Cultivation

The British expended considerable time and energy in investing and attempting to preserve certain aspects of communal possession and in preventing people from alienating communal land among the tribals (Thangchungnunga, 1993). When the local authorities constructed political system (which regulates the distribution of land), there was a noticeable shift from communal forms of possession to private ownership of land. This change had attributed in a general way to the development of commodity production and the breakdown of traditional labour pattern (Clarke, 1980). When cash was injected into the economy of the hill people by providing employment, people began to produce marketable commodity which gave rise to the development of private property. By the beginning of the present century, people in Mizoram started to plant orange gardens along the Tlawng River precisely because this river was the main line of communication with the rest of the country and market was easily available for the product. Thus, the process of land occupation was associated with the incorporation of a community into a monetised economy.

There was discontinuity in the development of land system in Mizoram as a result of the establishment of colonial state and the introduction of a new political system after independence. Where land is possessed communally, production agents cannot be said to possess land, but only to have access to it under definite conditions (Clarke, 1980). Access to land

and control over production process constituted land rights in the pre-colonial era, and production agents had access to land as independent producers under conditions defined by the rules of communal possession. When there was a transition of administrative power from primitive chieftainship to the British, that system continued but with the added administrative power to allocate land for permanent holding.

Even though there were instances where large scale plantation of orange entails fixing of the land in use, this did not represent a major departure from the existing mode of access to land. In the same way, tea, coffee, and tree plantation were steadily being practised by the cultivators. These types of plantations are permanent tree crops which are harvestable from their fifth year or so. Such permanent crops were regarded as the property of the producer and that planter was given exclusive rights over the particular plot of land in which the plantation is done. Thus, while there was no formal change in the allocation of land, the mode of distribution was altered. Such a system of retaining private rights in land occupation still exists in the rural sector. Our survey data, during January 2014, from 210 households in rural areas showed that around 62.85 per cent of the cultivable lands are in the form of VC Pass, which does not have any legal standpoint because the VCs are not entitled to allot such lands. However, these lands practically belong to these households and nobody challenge their ownership status. They claim exclusive rights over the land, though they are not yet recognised by the State Revenue Department through a Land Settlement Certificate (LSC).

The Survey Report of the 70th National Sample Survey (NSS) in 2013 stated that "a plot of land was considered owned by the household if permanent heritable possession, with or without the right to transfer the title, was vested in a member or members of the households." On the basis of the report on Land Holdings and Livestock of the NSS 37th Round, 9.7 per cent of the rural households of Mizoram were estimated to be landless households in 1983. The percentage of landless rural households significantly decreased to 2.34 per cent and 0.75 per cent in 2003 and 2013 respectively, according to the report of 70th NSS Round. In this NSS Round, all rural households having land less than 0.002 hectares were categorised as landless. Given the scanty spread of the population with a density of 52 persons per square kilometre, landlessness does not appear to be a big problem in rural areas of Mizoram till today.

According to the different agricultural censuses undertaken since 1976-77 till 2010-11, the total number of agricultural landholding, as presented in Table 2.2, has significantly increased from 48679 in 1976-77 to 91880 in 2010-11. According to the definition of the Agricultural Census, agricultural landholding is a land which is used wholly or partly for agricultural production and is operated as one technical unit by one person alone or with others without regards to the title, legal form, size, or location. Thus, land operated by an individual which may be called private land, whether with legal entitlement or not, has increased consistently during the last 30 years. As noted earlier, jhum land is meant for cultivation of one year beyond which the cultivator cannot claim ownership or entitlement. Agricultural holding here means land where the household can claim ownership, whether in legal form or not, and thus, they could be considered as private land. Since settled cultivation is directly associated with the emergence of private land, the trend observed in Table 2.2 is a clear indication of movement of the people from shifting to settled cultivation.

Table 2.2
Number of Agricultural Holdings in Mizoram (Agricultural Census)

Year	*Marginal*	*Small*	*Semi-Medium*	*Medium*	*Large*	*All sizes*
No. of Holdings						
1976-77	16682	19622	10586	1688	101	48679
1980-81	15651	19146	10380	1399	21	46597
1985-86	20692	18098	10967	1284	81	51122
1990-91	28538	23039	8736	717	--	61030
1995-96	27674	25656	11752	730	9	65821
2000-01	33695	27973	12539	1258	58	75523
2005-06	43382	31061	13744	1443	36	89666
2010-11	50210	29753	9922	1731	264	91880
Percentage share						
1976-77	34.27	40.31	21.75	3.47	0.21	100
1980-81	33.59	41.09	22.28	3.00	0.05	100
1985-86	40.48	35.40	21.45	2.51	0.16	100
1990-91	46.76	37.75	14.31	1.17	0.00	100
1995-96	42.04	38.98	17.85	1.11	0.01	100
2000-01	44.62	37.04	16.60	1.67	0.08	100
2005-06	48.38	34.64	15.33	1.61	0.04	100
2010-11	54.65	32.38	10.80	1.88	0.29	100

Source: Directorate of Economics & Statistics, *Statistical Abstract of Mizoram, 2015*, Govt. of Mizoram.

Agricultural holdings are divided into five categories as marginal (below 1 ha), small (1-2 ha), semi-medium (2-4 ha), medium (4-10 ha) and large (above 10 ha). In Mizoram, agricultural holding is tending towards marginal size as the share of marginal holdings has increased consistently over the years while other sizes of holdings (small, semi-medium, medium, and large) are showing more or less declining trends. The trend observed here is a result of the fragmentation of landholding over the years, in which increased population pressure on land is the biggest candidate for its cause.

Judging from the widespread existence of land rights in the form of permanent holding, the land system in Mizoram is far from being communal in nature. Meanwhile, the households identified as landless are by no means excluded from access to communally owned lands for jhum cultivation. The granting of exclusive rights of access to particular portions of a community's territory may be compatible with a definite form of communal possession. In this sense, the exclusive right of ownership is limited to an act of distribution of a communal territory among the members of the community. Here, community implies a village community within a well defined boundary line of land. However, the establishment of statutory rights over land creates a crucial condition for the dissolution of communal territory from within.

A private property right in land implies the right to dispose of land but this disposal right does not necessarily create a market for land, although it is an essential condition for the creation of such market (Clarke, 1980). Till the 1980s, sale of uncultivated land seldom took place in rural areas while flat land fields of rice and plantation plots were bought and sold frequently. Like other North Eastern States, selling and buying of land, including uncultivated land, have become very common nowadays in Mizoram with the improvement of road communication in different parts of the state. The situation is more prevalent near the state's capital and the low lying flat lands mostly in the areas neighbouring Assam state. Land that was once considered a livelihood is now a commodity that can be bought and sold. The main reason people cite for selling their land is the need of money for medical care and children's education. This results in internal land alienation within the tribe (Shimray, 2008). The emergence of land market merits special attention because those who can buy land are the richer class, and if unchecked, landholding will become concentrated in the hands of the few.

2.5. Land Use Change in Mizoram

Due to the absence of land use data that is presented continuously, it is very difficult to examine what changes have taken place in the scenario of agricultural land use in Mizoram. The first land use statistics was presented in the Report of Census of India 1961, but no record could be found thereafter. The methodology adopted to present land use statistics after Mizoram became a full-fledged state is significantly different from the one that was used in 1951. So, the figures are not compatible with the current data. In spite of this fact, it was attempted to examine the changes in agricultural land use through the available data. The land utilisation statistics of Mizoram in 1951 is presented in Table 2.3. Agriculture claims the largest share of land use and is the most important factor in deciding land use pattern. The land utilisation statistics of the Mizo District in the 1961 Census showed that the total cultivable area in 1951 was 1200.241 thousand hectares which accounted for 57 per cent of the total geographical area. This high proportion of land available for agricultural use was either fallow or waste land which is directly linked with the prevailing jhum system.

Table 2.3
Land Utilisation Statistics in Mizoram, 1951

Sl. No.	Type of Forest	Area (in Sq. Km)
A	**State Owned Forest**	6192.08
	1. Riverine Reserved Forest	1832.50
	2. Inner Line Reserved Forest	570.00
	3. Roadside Reserved Forest	97.20
	4. Other Reserved Forest	1963.63
	5. Wildlife Protected Areas	1728.75
B	**District Council Forests**	**2562.00**
C	**Total Reserved Forest**	**8754.08**

Source: As Reported in Census of India 1961 (cited by Thangchungnunga, 1993).
NR: Not Reported.

The North Eastern Council (NEC), Government of India, Shillong presented a more or less comparable land use data in its Basic Statistics of North Eastern Region published in 1992 and 2015.The NEC used the data of Ministry of Agriculture, Government of India as a source. The change in agricultural land use during 23 years from 1987-88 and 2010-11 is presented in Table 2.4. It can be observed that area put to non-agricultural use

Table 2.4
Land Use Change in Mizoram

Sl. No.	*Land Use*	*'000 Hectares*	
		1987-88	*2010-11*
1.	Total Geographical Area	2108	2108
2.	Reporting Area for Land Utilisation	2102	2101
3.	Forest Area	1303	1585
4.	Area put to Non-agricultural Uses	10	87
5.	Barren and Uncultivable Land	201	8
6.	Total Area not available for cultivation	211	95
7.	Permanent Pastures and other grazing land	4	5
8.	Cultivable waste land	74	39
9.	Other uncultivable land	3	7
10.	Current Fallows	183	66
11.	Fallow other than current fallow	259	181
12.	Net area sown	65	361

Source: Basic Statistics of North Eastern Region (1992 & 2015), North Eastern Council (NEC), Government of India, Shillong.

increased more than seven times during this period, which is justifiable due to population pressure on land, urbanisation, increasing developmental activities, etc. The net sown area also increased by more than four times, while other land use categories recorded a decreasing trend (47 per cent for waste land, and 96 per cent for barren and uncultivable land). The increasing net cultivation area with declining areas of unutilised lands may be interpreted as a result of land reclamation for cultivation during this period. At the same time, forest area increased from 1303 thousand hectares to 1585 thousand hectares (i.e. 21.64 per cent) during this period.

2.6. Concluding Notes

Land forms an integral part of the traditional Mizo society where every family practised shifting cultivation. The village chief was the absolute authority in respect to land management especially for the allotment of jhum land among the citizens. However, he is restricted by customary practices. Following the establishment of Mizo District Council, the power of the chiefs was abolished and a democratically elected Village Council came up, thus changing the modus operandi of land allotment for jhum land from the traditionally practised form based on social status to a simple draw of lot. The management of community land, in which shifting cultivation is practised, that used to be at the hands of the village chief became the responsibility of the Village Council.

The process of movement of the people from the practice of shifting cultivation to a settled one began with the introduction of settled cultivation by the state government through various developmental programmes. Private lands emerged rapidly, while the tendency of marginalisation of holdings can be clearly observed. At the same time, land market, where relatively richer sections of the society buy plots of land from the poor due to one reason or the other, also emerged following the improvement of road communication. With the enactment of various Acts and Rules by the government from time to time, the entire gamut of land tenure is now at the hands of the state government except for the VCs who are allowed to allot land for shifting cultivation for a period of one year after getting prior permission from the Revenue Department. Land resource management traditionally done at the village has now completely vanished and replaced by a system where the state government has full authority. The village council is not empowered to perform the task of land management. In view of the emergence of land markets, it is necessary to involve and empower the village authority (VC) on land resource management, without which prevention of land concentrating in the rich class would be a difficult task.

3

EMERGENCE OF LAND USE POLICIES

3.1. Introduction

The subject matter of jhum cultivation (shifting cultivation) has become a subject of debate among foresters, ecologists, economists, and policy makers (Leblhuber, *et al.*, 2012). The main contention is that it is the leading cause of land degradation (Lianzela, 1997; Maithani, 2005) that has constantly declined the agricultural productivity and thus income of the farmers (Sati and Rinawma, 2014). On the other hand, some scholars believe that it is a major source of livelihood of the people and a way of life for them. Jhumming is more than an occupation in Mizoram; it is a lifestyle and is an integral part of the socio-cultural life (Garbyal, 1999). However, with increase in population, the jhum cycle has shortened and its productivity has fallen, at the same time having devastating impact on the environment as a result of land degradation, silting of rivers, loss of fertility, landslips, and erosion. Despite its strong attachment to the socio-cultural life of the tribal population, famers have started feeling the pressure of growing population and shortening of the shifting cultivation cycle (Maithani, 2005). It is universally agreed that the jhumming is a primitive and unproductive method of cultivation (Garbyal, 1999), and it has become imperative to control it, which would not only improve the ecological quality but also enhance crop productivity (Sati and Rinawma, 2014).

Although shifting cultivation has been practised in Mizoram from time immemorial and by almost the entire population of the state, its adverse impact on the environment was never felt. Till the mid-1950s, there was no realisation that the damage to the top soil formed by hundreds of years of slow natural process would create any problem to the people (Lawma, 1991). With the establishment of Mizo District Council in 1952 after independence and its subsequent upgradation to Union Territory status in 1972, the need to switch the jhumia families to settled cultivation was seriously felt by the government. Thus, control of jhum cultivation became essential for the economic development of Mizoram and the other hill areas of North East India.

The first scheme named '*Garden Colony*' was launched on a small scale in 1978. Farmers who participated in this scheme were given cash assistance for clearing land and digging pits. They also received free planting materials. Subsequently, orchards became the principal component of more comprehensive programmes for jhum control, funded by both the centre and the state (Singh, 1996). Continuing its efforts to control jhum cultivation, the government implemented *New Land Use Policy* (NLUP) in the state in 1984. After Mizoram attained statehood in 1986, the initiative for jhum control was carried on by the new government of Mizo National Front which implemented Jhum Control Programme in 1987.

This chapter presents an account of the three major programmes implemented in Mizoram to abolish the practice of shifting cultivation during what may be called a *transitional period,* from 1977-78 to the later part of 1980s when the Mizoram was elevated to full-fledged State from the status of Union Territory. However, there are two serious problems limiting the reliability of the analysis. First is the lack of reliable data and proper records. There are no official publications regarding these schemes covering the entire period of study and so, we have to rely on various research papers, published and unpublished, which showed varying data. Secondly, lack of assessment or evaluation report officially made to show the performance of the scheme in achieving its desired objectives has limited the space for generating meaningful conclusion regarding the schemes. Nevertheless, attempt was made to present a true and unbiased view for the same as far as possible.

3.2. Garden Colony

In view of the rapid deterioration of the fertility of land due to prolonged practice of shifting cultivation and decreasing jhum cycle with population growth, the state government introduced several schemes of land development from the Fifth Plan period (i.e. 1974-79) onward. These schemes include land reclamation, settlement of jhumias on settled farming, soil amelioration, and improvement and terracing of hill slope lands (Thangchungnunga, 1997). It was also mentioned in the draft paper of the Sixth Plan that assistance would be extended to those who take up the following activities:

1. Reclamation of hilly land by introducing terraced cultivation at the rate of 80 per cent subsidy, subject to a maximum limit of Rs. 1,900 per hectare.
2. Reclamation of valley land at 50 per cent subsidy, to the extent of Rs. 1,500 per hectare.
3. Supply of agricultural inputs at 50 per cent subsidy.
4. Supply of planting materials free of cost or through grants of financial assistance to those who are settled under the scheme of "Garden Colony".
5. Construction of agricultural link roads at the cost of Rs. 7,000 per km.
6. Providing irrigation facilities at 50 per cent subsidy.

During the Annual Plan of 1977-78, the Government of Mizoram brought out a sponsored project of '*Garden Colony*' scheme. Under this scheme, it was intended to colonise several families in a compact area of settlement so that they might confine themselves to horticultural cultivation. It was expected that this would ultimately lead them to abandon the primitive jhum culture. The physical achievement of Garden Colony in the first two years of its implementation is presented in Table 3.1.

Financial assistance to households settled under 'Garden Colony' spread over a period of five years in a phased manner. The projected expenditure for horticultural development under the scheme is presented in Table 3.2. At the same time, cultivation of wet rice, of potato, and terracing of hill slopes were other important schemes which were phased for three years, as shown in Table 3.3. In each of these schemes, the government's financial involvement was limited to Rs. 15,000 per family.

Table 3.1
Physical Achievements of Garden Colony

Year	No. of Villages	Area Covered in Hectares	No. of Families	No. of Seedlings Distributed
1977-78	10	200	100	1,95,659
1978-79	31	1445	1445	6,38,945

Source: Department of Agriculture, "Notes on Agriculture, 1981" Government of Mizoram (cited Thangchungnunga, 1996).

Table 3.2
Year-Wise Phasing of Expenditure on Horticultural Development during the Sixth Plan

Sl. No.	Year	Expenditure (Rs.)
1.	1st year	3450.00
2.	2nd year	6050.00
3.	3rd year	2100.00
4.	4th year	900.00
5.	5th year	2000.00
	Total	**14,500.00**

Source: Sixth Five Year Plan, Government of Mizoram (cited Thangchungnunga, 1997).

Table 3.3
Government's Scheme of Financial Assistance for 'Garden Colony' Beneficiaries

Sl. No	Year	Expenditure (Rs.)
1.	1st year	4270.00
2.	4th year	10130.00
3.	5th year	600.00
	Total	**15,000.00**

Source: Sixth Five Year Plan, Government of Mizoram (cited Thangchungnunga, 1997).

Though the scheme was actually implemented with concerted effort on the part of the government as could be seen from the physical achievements in Table 3.1, it is difficult to examine its impact due to the unavailability of official records on it. No effort on its monitoring and evaluation was found to have taken place either. As the flow of expenditure on the development of the scheme was distributed year-wise in a pre-assigned order, the programme lacked fixation of target to be achieved within a stipulated time (Thangchungnunga, 1997). Further, there was no clear basis for identification of the beneficiaries for this scheme, leaving it to the responsibility of the concerned government officials. Following the defeat of the ruling People Conference (PC) party (who initiated the scheme) in the General Elections of 1984, the Garden Colony scheme was replaced by the New Land Use Policy (NLUP).

3.3. Concept of NLUP

Although the policy documents of NLUP issued from time to time did not provide clear cut conceptual definition, it can be gauged from its objectives and targeted groups. The main objective of the scheme was abolition of shifting (jhum) cultivation by providing the jhumia families permanent and sustainable means of livelihood, while also increasing the forest cover. It is a policy with an objective to put an end to the practice of jhumming by providing alternative land based permanent occupations and stable income to the families practising jhumming in rural areas thereby raising their standard of living (Garbyal, 1999). NLUP may, thus, be defined as a comprehensive strategy of the state government to put an end to the practice of shifting cultivation by providing sustainable permanent means of livelihood to the jhumia families, to provide better livelihood opportunities to the poor, and to increase the forest cover to ensure ecological balance in the long run.

The policy encompassed simultaneous attempts on progressive reduction of areas under jhum cultivation and its complete abolition in some future date; allotment of suitable land to individual rural households for permanent cultivation and utilisation on the basis of working capacity of the family; promotion of wet rice cultivation for self-sufficiency in food production; and preservation and protection of land areas other than those allotted for permanent cultivation so as to keep significantly large areas under forest cover. The aims and objectives of the programme are as follows:

(a) to put an end to the practice of jhumming (shifting cultivation),
(b) to induce each jhumia family to take up alternative permanent means of livelihood under either agriculture or industry or animal husbandry sectors on the land allotted for the purpose,

(c) to take up wet rice cultivation in all the potential flat lands in order to promote self-sufficiency in food production,
(d) to protect and afforest lands other than those earmarked for NLUP, and
(e) to provide marketing outlets for produces.

The policy set out a clear target group to be covered, while also making criteria for exclusion of some families from the scheme. The target groups were:

(a) families who depend upon jhumming for their livelihood, and
(b) families other than jhumias having no permanent means of livelihood but consisting of able-bodied members capable of physical labour.

At the same time, families belonging to the following categories were automatically excluded:

(i) families having permanent source of regular income, e.g. government employees, commercial business dealers, registered contractors, full time mission workers, employees of government aided schools, etc.,
(ii) families having a permanent farm with potential of yielding sufficient returns to sustain a family,
(iii) families holding developed irrigated land but cultivating through hired labourers instead of engaging in self-cultivation,
(iv) families who are permanently engaged in livestock or any industrial venture deriving sufficient income.

3.4. Implementation of NLUP during 1984-87

In order to control and replace the primitive agricultural practice of shifting cultivation (Lawma, 1991) and to protect the land from degradation and to promote productivity (Upadhyaya and Jha, 1997), a meeting of the Council of Ministers dated 24 November 1984 decided to introduce a new scheme called New Land Use Policy (Zoramchhana, 2000). With the guidelines of the project having been laid down by the meeting, the scheme was introduced in the state with immediate effect. It was initially expected to be implemented till 1989. However, when the Congress (Indian National Congress) government was replaced by the Mizo National Front (MNF) in 1987 following the Mizo Peace Accord, 1986, the programme suffered a serious setback. Consequently, the programme was implemented for three years only, from 1984-85 to 1986-87.

The scheme was implemented through several state government departments like Environment and Forest, Soil and Water Conservation, and Agriculture, coordinated through Rural Development Department. Different departments identified families to rehabilitate them on settled farming, plantation, etc. They had different orientation and approaches but in each case, financial support to the families for a few years is assured and the support was up to Rs. 3,000 per family.

The operational procedures and measures adopted by the government in the implementation of the New Land Use Policy (NLUP) as presented in the policy guidelines may be narrated as follows:

(1) Firstly, survey and identification of both the existing area under wet rice cultivation (WRC) and other lands suitable for WRC. The survey report would be recorded village-wise and would include those individual/private lands lying unused for potential WRC.
(2) Secondly, private land owners would be given one year period to make use of the land, failing which either their land passes would be cancelled or the land may be acquired by the government for allotment to other suitable families.
(3) Thirdly, the land survey reports would be shown in survey maps and the allotment to different families would be made in consultation and cooperation of the people concerned.
(4) In view of the shortages of suitable land for WRC, other areas of 'compact land' would be identified and surveyed and then allotted to suitable families for development on permanent basis. In this case, the land may be utilised for other purposes including animal husbandry, fishery development, horticulture, forestry, etc.
(5) For every area of land allotted to each individual family, the agency appointed by the government, in cooperation with the people concerned, will prepare a project report for the development and scientific use of the land so allotted. The project report should include the nature and type of land use suggested, cost and probable

assistance that may be granted by the government and other financial institutions, and the amount of contribution required from the family. The project report should indicate the schedule of operation of the project, preferably not more than five years duration.

(6) To ensure the feasibility of the project, a model village would be selected from each development block for which a team of officers from different departments such as Agriculture, Animal Husbandry, Revenue, Industry, Forest, etc. will draw up a project report after proper survey and identification. This would serve as a model or demonstration project for other villages of the area.

(7) The area of land to be allotted to the individual family would depend on the capacity of such family to make use of the land and also the availability of assistance from the government and other financial institutions.

(8) The project report for each individual family should be kept in both the office of the Development Commissioner and the Deputy Commissioner for ready reference, and a certain degree of flexibility and scope for minor modifications would be provided in the course of implementation.

(9) Land would be allotted to the individual family at first instance on 'lease' basis for a period of ten years during which no transfer or sale of the land is allowed. Permanent allotment would be accorded only after the land is fully utilised for the purpose it is allotted. Besides, no compensation or any other legal claim would be entertained as and when the government requires the land for road construction, development programmes, etc.

The scheme had a target of 20,000 families of the total of 60,000 jhumia families for settlement on about 21,000 hectares in three years. The selected families would be allotted the required land on long lease basis for carrying out settled agriculture, horticulture, dairy farming, pig farming, raising plantation crops, etc. (Maithani, 2005). It was expected that all lands, other than town and village lands and the land allotted to individual families for permanent cultivation, be notified as natural and protected forest. The villagers were allowed to collect fuel wood, fodder, and small timber for home consumption but not for commercial purposes.

To ensure better coordination, supervision, and utilisation of funds among the concerned departments, a Committee consisting of the Directors of Agriculture, Animal Husbandry and all heads of the departments involved in the scheme was formed under the chairmanship of Development Commissioner. The main task of the Committee was to prepare the framework of the scheme and to identify the planning provisions for every year. This task was to be worked out and readied by the 15th of April every year.

The project report should clearly indicate the schemes and purposes for which the assistance of the government is provided. The copy of the statement would be attached along with the sanction order and a copy should be given to the coordinating agency. Such records as maintained by the coordinating agency would be updated every year by the month of April. The Deputy Commissioner (DC) or his representatives would verify the registers maintained in every village and also conduct physical verification of all the individual projects taken up with the assistance of the government under the scheme at least once a year. Further, each beneficiary family was required to engage itself in the actual work and no outside labour or daily wage earner were to be employed on a regular basis.

3.5. Physical and Financial Achievement of NLUP (1984-87)

The state government targeted to cover 5000 families in 1984-85, with an aim to cover additional 10,000 families every succeeding year so that all the 60,000 families would be brought under the scheme in the course of the six years. The year wise physical achievements, i.e. families brought under NLUP, among the participating departments (Line Departments) are presented in Table 3.4.

A total of 15076 families against the target of 20000 families were covered under the scheme during the first three years of its implementation. The number of beneficiaries increased from 4269 in 1984-85 to 6428 in 1985-86 and 4379 in 1986-87. Department-wise distribution may further be sub-divided into three broad sectors as agriculture and allied, forest, and animal husbandry. It can be derived that the contribution of agriculture and allied sector, consisting of Agriculture, Soil and Water Conservation, Sericulture and Fisheries, is largest at 56.85 per cent followed by Forest (29.74 per cent) and Animal Husbandry (13.41 per cent). It may be noted

Table 3.4
Physical Achievement (No. of Beneficiaries) of New Land Use Policy (1984-1987)

Sl. No.	*Department*	*No. of Families*				*Share (Percent)*
		1984-85	*1985-86*	*1986-87*	*Total*	
1.	Forest	1259	3224	–	4483	29.74
2.	Animal Husbandry & Veterinary	226	796	1000	2022	13.41
3.	Fisheries	–	112	–	112	0.74
4.	Soil & Water Conservation	946	414	940	2300	15.26
5.	Agriculture	1069	1788	1773	4630	30.71
6.	Sericulture	769	94	666	1529	10.14
	Total	**4269**	**6428**	**4379**	**15076**	**100**

Source: Department of Rural Development, Mizoram, Aizawl (Lawma, 1991).

that horticulture, which is one of the major economic sectors, is now clubbed under Agriculture Department. The year-wise number of families presented in Table 3.4 shows that substantial number of families were covered by Agriculture, Animal Husbandry, Soil and Water Conservation, and Sericulture throughout the three years. However, there were gaps when no beneficiaries were selected for the departments of Forest and Fisheries during the same period.

The NLUP was implemented through a centrally sponsored scheme of Social Forestry (Zoramchhana, 2000) and Plan Budget of the state government. The year-wise expenditure for NLUP scheme among each of the participating departments is presented in Table 3.5. A total amount of Rs. 344.2 lakh was spent for the scheme from 1984-85 to 1986-87. The annual expenditure for the programme increased from Rs. 87.42 lakh in 1984-85 to Rs. 128.28 lakh in 1985-86 and Rs. 128.5 lakh in 1986-87. The percentage share of each department shows the dominance of Forest Department which constituted 32.88 per cent followed by Agriculture (26.14 per cent), while it was lowest for Fisheries (0.98 per cent). At the same time, agriculture and allied sector constituted the largest share among the three major economic sectors. This sector constituted 55.13 per cent of the total expenditure, while it was 32.88 per cent and 12 per cent for Forest and Animal Husbandry, respectively. Further, as there were no beneficiaries selected under Forest Department in 1986-87 and under Fisheries in 1984-85 and 1986-87, no expenditure was recorded for these years.

Table 3.5
Expenditure under New Land Use Policy (1984-1987)

Sl. No	Department	Total Expenditure (Rs. in lakhs)				Share (Percent)
		1984-85	1985-86	1986-87	Total	
1.	Forest	16.44	96.72	–	113.16	32.88
2.	Animal Husbandry & Veterinary	5.65	5.65	30	41.3	12.00
3.	Fisheries	–	3.36	–	3.36	0.98
4.	Soil & Water Conservation	29.39	15.05	25.33	69.77	20.27
5.	Agriculture	32.1	4.68	53.19	89.97	26.14
6.	Sericulture	3.84	2.82	19.98	26.64	7.74
	Total	**87.42**	**128.28**	**128.5**	**344.2**	**100**

Source: Department of Rural Development, Mizoram, Aizawl (Lawma, 1991).

Table 3.6
Expenditure Per Beneficiary under New Land Use Policy (1984-1987)

Sl. No.	Department	Expenditure per Beneficiary (Rs)				Total Exp. (Rs. Lakhs)
		1984-85	1985-86	1986-87	Total	
1.	Forest	1306	3000	–	2524	113.16
2.	Animal Husbandry & Veterinary	2500	710	3000	2043	41.3
3.	Fisheries	–	3000	–	3000	3.36
4.	Soil & Water Conservation	3107	3635	2695	3033	69.77
5.	Agriculture	3003	262	3000	1943	89.97
6.	Sericulture	499	3000	3000	1742	26.64
	Total	**2048**	**1996**	**2934**	**2283**	**344.2**

Source: Calculated from Table 3.1 & 3.2.

To have a better understanding of the achievement of the government in the provision of assistance under NLUP, an attempt was made to work out the amount expended per family (beneficiary) which is presented in Table 3.6. The average expenditure for all departments turned out to be Rs. 2,283 per beneficiary. It was highest under Soil and Water Conservation (Rs. 3,033), and Fisheries (Rs. 3,000), while it was lowest in case of Sericulture (Rs. 1,742) and Agriculture departments (Rs. 1,943). The financial achievement as indicated by expenditure per beneficiary was well below the target because the original targeted value was Rs. 3,000 per family. The overall financial achievement is estimated to be only 76.10 per cent of the target, which is lowest for Sericulture (58.08 per cent) and highest in case of Soil and Water Conservation (101.12 per cent). Notably, the target was achieved by two departments — Soil and Water Conservation, and Fisheries. However, the actual amount that reached the beneficiaries would be much lower if the expenditure incurred on administration and direction of the programme is taken into account.

3.6. Critical Evaluation of NLUP (1984-1987)

It could be observed from the preceding tables that the government of Mizoram has shown commendable efforts to put an end to the primitive practice of shifting cultivation by introducing the NLUP programme. There were notable physical and financial achievements. The total number of jhum families covered under the programme during the three years of its implementation was 15076, and the total expenditure for the entire project was Rs. 344.2 lakh. Having examined the progressive implementation of the programme, it is pertinent to study its impact. However, an in-depth analysis could not be undertaken due to unavailability of comprehensive data. So, the analysis was conducted on the basis of two sources: (i) Data from Statistical Handbook of Mizoram; and (ii) published and unpublished records and observations of individual researchers.

Given the limited set of data available for the analysis on the success of the programme, we are compelled to utilise the changes in the macro level data on the status of agriculture in Mizoram during the study period. There were two clear trends on the agricultural scenario implicating the impact of NLUP during the period. Firstly, as reduction of jhumming practice was the main objective of the programme, the starting point of the impact analysis should be on the reduction of jhum areas and production. It can be observed from Table 3.7 that the cultivated area of paddy (rice) under jhum cultivation decreased from 41280.7 hectares in 1983-84 to 38892.5 hectares in 1986-87 and 36616 hectares in 1988-89. That is, there was 11.30 per cent decrease in the area under shifting cultivation between 1983-84 and 1988-89. Similarly, the jhum production declined (by 36.83 per cent) from 25573.39 MT in 1983-84 to 34993 MT in 1988-89. If we compare the increase in areas and production of rice under WRC between 1983-84 and 1988-89, it was 99.87 per cent and 115.49 per cent respectively. This may be construed as the result of effort through NLUP during this period. Meanwhile, the population of the state had increased by around 40 per cent from 493757 in 1981 to 689756 in 1991. Taking into account the

Table 3.7
Change in Area and Production of Paddy in Mizoram: Pre and Post NLUP (1983-1989)

Year	*Area (Hectares)*		*Production (MT)*	
	Jhum	*WRC*	*Jhum*	*WRC*
1983-84	41280.7	6390	25573.39	11137.53
1984-85	40000	7486	43593.15	14826.14
1985-86	45920	9092	55209	9571
1986-87	38892.5	9451.5	49622.5	19121
1987-88	37803	10661	—	—
1988-89	36616	12772	34993	24000
Total change (%)	**–11.30**	**99.87**	**36.83**	**115.49**

Source: Statistical Handbook of Mizoram (Various Issues), Directorate of Economics. & Statistics., Government. of Mizoram.

population increase side by side with the reduction of areas under jhum cultivation, it can be concluded that substantial number of families moved out of the practice of shifting cultivation during this decade. Thus, the implementation of NLUP as a means of jhum control was a significant factor for reducing jhumming practice, which was its main objective.

Secondly, change in the cropping pattern is another area where the impact of NLUP is evident. It can be observed from Table 3.8 that the cultivated areas for the other jhum-based crops experienced a declining trend, while major crops under settled cultivation showed an increasing trend. The cultivated area for chilli and ginger decreased significantly between 1985 and 1988, while areas under maize decreased from 4872 Ha in 1985 to 4248 Ha in 1987 and increased to 5911 Ha in 1988. At the same time, there was significant increase in areas under cultivation of orange, banana, and pineapple, while for sugarcane it increased from 617.3 Ha in 1985 to 935 Ha in 1987 but decreased to 544.1 Ha in 1988. The same trend can also be seen in production. To further justify this observation, the change in the percentage composition of jhum crops and settled cultivation crops may be examined. The percentage share of area cover for the jhum crops studied viz., chilli, ginger, and maize, and shown in Table 3.8, declined consistently from 77.69 per cent in 1985 to 64.52 per cent in 1988, while the share of other crops (settled cultivation) increased consistently from 22.31 per cent in 1985 to 35.48 per cent in 1988. Similarly, the production share of the former decreased from 64.31 per cent to 47.77 per cent, while that of settled crops increased from 35.69 per cent to 54.23 per cent during the same period. This is a clear indication of change in the cropping patterns that accompanied the implementation of NLUP in Mizoram from 1984-85 till 1986-87.

Table 3.8
Area and Production of Major Crops in Mizoram (1985-1988)

Crops	*Area (Hectares)*				*Production (MT)*			
	1985	*1986*	*1987*	*1988*	*1985*	*1986*	*1987*	*1988*
Chillies	2525	2329	2481	2089.46	2238	3209	3300	1952
Ginger	1646	1139	1244	1234.46	6906	6492	4500	8436.8
Maize	4872	4000	4248	5911	6435	6520	7500	9500
Orange	746	1590	1664	1889.9	—	—	—	—
Banana	873	1500	1171	1802.11	5000	6000	7784	13292.85
Pineapple	360	400	520	842.46	964	5200	6000	3799.2
Sugarcane	617.3	588	935	544.1	2680.7	5870	2956	6470.54
Total	**11639.3**	**11546**	**12263**	**14313.49**	**24223.7**	**33291**	**32040**	**43451.39**

Source: Statistical Handbook of Mizoram (Various Issues), Directorate of Economics. & Statistics., Government of Mizoram.

In spite of the declining jhum area and crop diversification towards off-jhum crops presented above, there were a number of issues pointed out by some researchers thus showing the poor performance of the scheme to achieve the desired objectives. Firstly, there was a big gap between the physical target and actual achievement. Only 15076 families against the target of 20000 families, i.e. 75.38 per cent were covered within three years; while assistance of only Rs. 2,283 per family on an average, including the administrative expenses, could be achieved against the target package of Rs. 3,000 per family showing a shortfall of around 24 per cent. Further, the amount of assistance given to the beneficiaries was too meagre if we account for the suggestion of the meeting of Board on Shifting Cultivation held in Kohima in 1985. The Board suggested that a minimum of at least Rs. 30,000 per family is required to serve any useful purpose in the resettlement programme of the jhumias (Lawma, 1991).

Secondly, large numbers of beneficiaries were not sincere in the development of their lands. Even though they made promises not to burn the forest, they did so anyway (Upadhyaya and Jha, 1997), and the financial assistance received for the purpose was spent obviously for conspicuous consumption (Lawma, 1991). Thirdly, there was a lot of slackness and inefficiency on the part of the government in respect of the effective implementation of the scheme. Formulation, monitoring, evaluation, and reporting of the scheme were not efficient. No guidelines were drawn for the guidance of field officers. As a result, selection of beneficiaries was faulty and the package of schemes was neither uniform nor focused on the needs and potential of the families covered under it (Maithani, 2005). There was an apparent haste to take the 100 per cent financing available with the Planning Commission for the purpose. While roping in new families, nothing was learnt from the experience of the old ones (Upadhyaya and Jha, 1997).

Lastly, absence of initiatives on land reforms would challenge the positive impact of the programme for the long run. As per the record of Directorate of Economics and Statistics in its Statistical Handbook of Mizoram, the number of Agricultural Land Passes for WRC, garden, fish ponds, etc. issued per year were 818 in 1986-87, 182 in 1989-90, 80 in 1990-91, 58 in 1991-92, 49 in 1994-95, and 186 in 1995-96. The policy guidelines envisioned that the beneficiary would be accorded permanent ownership once the plots were fully utilised for the purpose. There were significant differences in the number of Land Settlement Certificates (LSC) issued per year and the number of beneficiaries under NLUP since 1984. This trend suggests the situation where only a negligible number of beneficiaries could be settled in the land where they were given permanent entitlements in the form of LSC. This could be taken as a serious setback of the programme.

3.7. Jhum Control Project

In 1987, the Mizo National Front (MNF) took over the ministry from the Congress and replaced the NLUP with a centre-sponsored Jhum Control Project (JCP). The pilot project was implemented in Aibawk RD Block in 1987-88 and the scheme was extended to Tuipang RD Block the next year. However, the scale was curtailed as the National Development Council discontinued the Special Area Development Programme in eight states, including the Jhum Control Project in Mizoram (Singh, 2007). Thus, the project was not able to make much headway and was discontinued immediately without significant impact.

Information could be obtained from Aibawk RD Block only, in which 1936 beneficiaries from 16 villages participated. The aim of the project was to progressively reduce and replace jhumming till its complete abandonment by 1993. Horticulture was the most favoured option. Where topography permitted, WRC, bench terracing, contour bunding, and minor irrigation were to be introduced. Improved piggery, poultry and duck rearing, cattle development and upgradation of local cows were also planned. Crafts, such as carpentry, tailoring, and knitting were to be promoted. Departmental works were proposed for soil and water conservation, social forestry, roads, and other support infrastructure. Every family was a beneficiary under the programme, including those in government service. Of the 1936 participants, 47 per cent opted for horticulture, 20 per cent for animal husbandry, 10 per cent for WRC, 9 per cent for coffee plantation, 5 per cent for dry terrace cultivation, 5 per cent for sericulture, and 3 per cent for cottage industries (Singh, 2007). Assistance in cash and in kind was to the extent of Rs. 30,000 per family. The total project cost was estimated to be 5.30 crore and was aiming at complete abolition of jhumming in the state by 1993 (Menon, 1988). However, the total financial achievements and actual amount of assistance provided to the beneficiaries could not be ascertained clearly from the available sources.

3.8. Conclusion

The impact of traditional practice of shifting cultivation on the natural environment and the resultant decline in land fertility following increasing population pressure on land had been recognised by the society as well as the government in Mizoram. Jhum control came to the fore in the policy debates since the beginning of 1980s. Consequently, a new programme primarily meant for abolition of shifting cultivation, christened as New Land Use Policy (NLUP), was launched by the government in 1984 and was implemented till it was replaced by another project called Jhum Control Project in 1987. Strong effort was shown by the government towards the success of NLUP. As many as 15076 jhum families were selected to be settled in the system of permanent cultivation under Agriculture, Forest, Sericulture, Soil and Water Conservation, Fisheries, and Animal Husbandry by providing cash assistance of Rs. 2,283 per beneficiary on an average during the three years.

Given the absence of comprehensive data for evaluation of its impact, the study relied on the changes in the scenario of the state agriculture whose data is available from the record of Economics and Statistics Department. It observed that the progressive implementation of NLUP was associated by a gradual shift of jhum families to other cultivation during the period of 1984-1988. The reduction of areas under shifting cultivation during the period was considered significant keeping in view the growth rate of the population (i.e. around 40 per cent between 1981 and 1991). Reduction of shifting cultivation was positively related to the increasing area and production of other crops like banana, orange, pineapple, sugarcane, etc. The share of these crops on the total agricultural production increased significantly.

However, one clear observation that came up from the analysis is that the amount of assistance given to the beneficiaries was too little to make any headway, while even the assistance was well below the targeted amount of Rs. 3,000 per family. The beneficiaries were also found to not have given dedicated effort to ensure the success of the scheme. They were reportedly using most of the assistance they had received under the scheme on other purposes, mostly for conspicuous consumption. Moreover, there was inefficiency in the coordination of works and its monitoring on the part of the state government departments. The failure of the government to ensure settlement of land allotted for NLUP against the provision of the policy objectives and operational guidelines appears to be a serious shortcoming. The problem can be seen from the fact that only a negligible number of families were given LSC even after 10 years. Thus, the programme could be hypothesised to operate in such a way as to dislocate the well-organised system of traditional shifting cultivation. In the villages where jhumming had been banned, people continued the practice covertly in small groups which showed lack of discipline and foresight of the village councils (Singh, 2007).

4

REVIVAL OF NLUP IN MIZORAM IN 1991

4.1. Introduction

Although the New Land Use Policy (NLUP) was started in 1984-85, it was discontinued before any significant achievement could be made due to a change in the Government in 1987 (Garbyal, 1999). The subsequent government of Mizo National Front (MNF) continued the effort of putting an end to the practice of shifting cultivation in a smaller scale by launching a new scheme called Jhum Control Project (JCP) in 1987-88. Unlike the NLUP scheme, it was initially implemented in one RD block (Aibawk) with an intention to expand it in other blocks. However the JCP could not make any significant impact due to a funding problem following the stoppage of financial support by National Development Council (NDC).

With the return of the Congress Party in the Ministry under Lal Thanhawla in 1989, the NLUP programme was revived with major improvements over the first attempt (Singh, 2007). The government decided to reorganise and enlarge the Rural Development Department by inducting officers and staff from nine departments that are directly concerned with the implementation of NLUP, i.e. departments of Agriculture, Soil and Water Conservation, Animal Husbandry, Sericulture, Industries, Fisheries, Forests, Information and Public Relations, and Finance and Accounts. A new Commissionerate was set up under a full-fledged Commissioner. The Rural Development (RD) Department started formulating the annual plan with effect from 1990-91 beginning with an outlay of Rs. 12 crore (Garbyal, 1999). Four RD blocks, namely West Phaileng, Reiek, Thingsulthliah, and Lungsen were initially brought under the programme. The project lasted till the financial year of 1996-97. This Chapter presents the different aspects of the implementation of NLUP in Mizoram since 1990-91 till 1996-97 based on the information obtained from various sources.

4.2. Operational Guidelines and Procedure

Under the NLUP, assistance was to be provided for each trade or occupation for a period of three years. The scheme was implemented as per the Calendar of Works wherein the chronological order of each phase of work was given and the beneficiaries were expected to strictly adhere to it. The programme was operated on a yearly basis, and all the Rural Development Blocks were expected to be covered by the end of the Eighth Five year Plan (1992-97). The criteria adopted for the selection of the development blocks was more or less the same as the one recommended by the National Commission on Agriculture (Lawma, 1991). They are:

(1) area where at least 85 per cent of the rural population are dependent on jhum cultivation and wherein, the jhum cycle was also fast declining,
(2) RD Blocks having international border were to be given preference with a view to check illegal infiltration and immigration from across the border,
(3) RD Blocks having potential for foodgrain production, and
(4) good communication network to facilitate marketing, supervision, and monitoring, etc.

After the state cabinet selected a block for the year, the RD Department staff should launch a public awareness campaign and prepare a list of bona fide beneficiaries in each village with the assistance of the Village Council (VC). Practically, the Block Development Officers (BDO) were given discretionary powers in the selection of beneficiaries (Maithani, 2005). In contrast to the Jhum Control Project, the beneficiaries were to be restricted to those practising shifting cultivation or those lacking permanent means of livelihood. However, the BDO was given discretionary powers in the beneficiary selection and finalisation of trade of each selected beneficiary

(Singh, 2007). As the VC could no longer make recommendations for land allotment to the Revenue Department, the BDO was empowered to allot suitable land for NLUP activities and to demarcate compact area for the scheme. Meanwhile, the Local Administration Department (LAD) placed a ban on jhumming in villages covered by the programme.

Assistance was in the form of either cash or kind, and its disbursement was witnessed by the VCs in their respective jurisdiction. The assistance was to be phased over two to three years, with a ceiling of Rs. 30,000 per family, relaxable by Rs. 5,000 in deserving cases. Before disbursements were made, the beneficiaries were required to give an undertaking to the effect that the grant and other assistances would not be diverted for other purposes, and in case they do, they would be debarred from further assistance. Given this background, the state government felt necessary that, for effective implementation of the programme, RD Department needed to be re-organised and enlarged into a Commissionerate. This Commissionerate consists of a Commissioner, officers, and staff from the concerned departments. The guidelines, aims, and objectives laid down were:

(1) to put an end to the practice of hill side jhum cultivation,
(2) to induce the jhumia families to take up alternative permanent means of livelihood under agriculture or industries or animal husbandry sectors,
(3) to take up WRC in all potential flat lands in order to promote self-sufficiency in food production,
(4) to protect and to intensify afforestation in the remaining lands other than those allotted for the programme, and
(5) to provide marketing outlet for produce from the programme.

The target group of the programme was clearly mentioned. They were mostly jhumia families and poor people who do not have permanent means of livelihood. At the same time, families belonging to the following categories would be automatically excluded from selection: families having permanent source of regular income; owning permanent farms with potential yield sufficient to sustain a family; holding developed irrigated land for WRC and cultivating through hired labourers; those permanently engaged in livestock rearing or any comparable industrial venture, and deriving sufficient income; and immigrant families, that had earlier received assistance under NLUP from some other development block.

The state government also laid down clear criteria about the misuse of the assistance. They were — migration of the beneficiaries without permission after receiving assistance; sale of assets created through the assistance; and diversion of the assistance to purposes other than those for which it is given. Penalty for the misuse of assistance were

(i) they might be barred from receiving assistance from the government in the future,
(ii) the value of the assistance already given, calculated on the basis of the prevailing market rate, would be recovered in full from the beneficiary, and
(iii) in case recovery was not feasible, other forms of punishment considered appropriate by the government would be awarded.

Submission of reports was of vital importance for the review and monitoring of the programme. The BDOs accordingly were to submit monthly and annual reports of the programme to the RD Department. With a view to create awareness among the general public, and to motivate different groups of officials involved in the implementation of the scheme, the department published magazines, folders, stickers, pamphlets, and leaflets with appropriate illustrations; and also organised plays and seminars on the subject. Considering the significance of spot verification for the success of the scheme, the BDOs assigned specific territorial units (called Circles) to the field functionaries, such as Extension Officers (EO) and Village Level Workers (VLW). The field functionaries would verify and inspect the beneficiaries within their respective circles and record their observations into their Vikas Patrikas on the spot (Das, 2004). Inspection reports were to be submitted by the EOs/VLWs to the BDOs; who would further submit the reports to the RD Department headquarters in Aizawl.

4.3. Main and Subsidiary Trades under NLUP

Unlike its predecessor in 1984, the programme was introduced in a form of *composite schemes* rather than a single scheme. This was done to overcome the problems faced by farmers who undertake activities with long gestation period. Thus, each principal (main) trade was linked to a subsidiary one that could yield quicker returns. Different trades under the scheme can be broadly categorised into three sectors, namely, (1) agriculture and allied sector, (2) animal husbandry and veterinary sector, and (3) industrial sector (especially cottage industries). These were the major sectors of rural economy that are closely related to land use and its changing patterns and overall integrated development of rural societies.

The agriculture and allied sector comprised of 28 main trades and five subsidiary trades. The main and subsidiary trades under this sector are presented in Table 4.1. To sustain the earning of income by the beneficiary during the gestation period of their main trade, an additional amount of assistance not exceeding Rs. 5,000 would be given for subsidiary trades. There were eight major trades and three subsidiary trades under the animal husbandry and veterinary sector. Unlike the agriculture and allied sector, a subsidiary trade was allotted specifically for a particular trade. For example, the allotted trades for piggery and sheep rearing are vegetables and piggery respectively. However, no subsidiary trade was allotted for dairying trade. Table 4.2 describes the details of trades under this sector.

Table 4.1
Statement of Main and Subsidiary Trades under Agriculture and Allied Sector

Main Trades			*Subsidiary Trades*
1. Mandarin Orange	11. Tea	21. Pisciculture	1. Vegetable Garden
2. Iskut (Squash)	12. Banana	22. Valencia	2. Piggery
3. Wet Rice Cultivation (WRC)	13. Passion Fruit	23. Mango	3. Poultry
4. Assam Lemon	14. Sericulture	24. Citronella	4. Betelvine
5. Pineapple	15. Apple	25. Coffee	5. Duckery
6. Hatkora	16. Grape	26. Betelvine	Note: No Subsidiary trade for Iskut (Squash) and Passion Fruit as these are quick yielding
7. Hill Terracing	17. Jamir	27. Arecanut	
8. Sugarcane	18. Kagji Lime	28. Pomelo	
9. Tung	19. Teak		
10. Coconut	20. Litchi		

Source: Manual for New Land Use Policy, Department of Rural Development, 1991.

Meanwhile, beneficiaries undertaking industrial trades were given freedom to choose any one of the subsidiary trades from piggery, poultry, and vegetable gardening. However, no subsidiary trade was given for carpentry. As presented in Table 4.3, there were 15 main trades and three subsidiary trades under industrial sector. Since distinction was made between

Table 4.2
Statement of Main and Subsidiary Trades under Animal Husbandry and Veterinary Sector

Main Trades	*Subsidiary Trades*
1. Hill Cattle/ Mithun	Vegetables
2. Dairying	—
3. Piggery	Vegetables
4. Goat Rearing	Piggery
5. Poultry	Vegetables
6. Rabbit Rearing	Vegetables
7. Duck Rearing	Vegetables & Piggery
8. Sheep Rearing	Piggery

Source: Manual for New Land Use Policy, Department of Rural Development, 1991.

Table 4.3
Statement of Main and Subsidiary Trades under Industrial Sector

Main Trades			*Subsidiary Trades*
1. Carpentry	2. Tailoring	3. Handloom	1. Piggery
4. Bakery	5. Shoe Repairing	6. Knitting	2. Poultry
7. Cane and Bamboo	8. Chow Making	9. Tinsmithy	3. Vegetables
10. Radio Repairing	11. Motor Workshop	12. Watch Repairing	*Note:* No Subsidiary trade for Carpentry
13. Arts & Painting	14. Black Smithy (Electrified and Non-electrified)		
15. Rice Huller (Electrified & Non-electrified)			

Source: Manual for New Land Use Policy, Department of Rural Development, 1991.

electrified and non-electrified in case of blacksmithy and rice huller, the number of main trades in practical sense was 17.

4.4. Progress of the Implementation

With an aim to cover all the 20 RD Blocks within the Eighth Five Year Plan (1992-97), the programme was implemented from the financial year of 1990-91. However, due to certain problems in the flow of fund, the programme was extended till the beginning of the Ninth Five Year Plan and was discontinued in 1998 (Zoramchhana, 2000). Rural development was the main guiding principle of the implementation of NLUP. There were two major aspects of its implementation. First, the choice of beneficiary was restricted to jhumia families or landless families so as to give them a piece of land for raising agricultural productivity and diversifying the rural livelihood activities in relation to the availability of local resources. Second, the agro-climatic and socio-economic factors of the land were considered for land allotment.

Initially, four RD Blocks, namely Thingsulthliah, West Phaileng, Reiek, and Lungsen, were covered with an outlay of Rs. 1,200 lakh and new blocks were added every year. Table 4.4 shows the progress of NLUP implementation among different RD blocks in Mizoram. A total of 12 blocks was covered between 1990-91 and 1996-97 with a total expenditure of Rs. 15,539 lakh. It is shown in this table that no new RD block was selected during 1992-93 as re-scrutiny of the programme was done and concentration was given to the on-going works. As the assistances to the beneficiaries were made on an instalment basis, the annual expenditure in a current year also included the expenditure on those that were covered in the preceding year.

Table 4.4
Year-Wise Coverage of RD Blocks under NLUP

Year	*RD Block Covered*	*Expenditure (Rs. in lakhs)*
1990-91	Thingsulthliah, West Phaileng, Reiek, and Lungsen	1200.00
1991-92	Thingdawl, and Zawlnuam	2070.00
1992-93	—	2220.00
1993-94	Serchhip, and East Lungdar	2770.00
1994-95	Khawzawl, and Lunglei	2479.00
1995-96	Tlangnuam	2500.00
1996-97	Ngopa	2300.00
	TOTAL	**15539.00**

Source: *Abstract of NLUP Beneficiaries*, Government of Mizoram, 1998.
Note: Annual Expenditure also includes the successive instalments given to the beneficiaries in the RD Blocks covered in the preceding years.

A total of 49023 beneficiaries (families) out of 109431 families from 12 RD blocks were covered under the scheme between 1990-91 and 1996-97. The number of beneficiaries was 44.80 per cent of the total number of households in the 12 Blocks. The percentage is lowest in Tlangnuam at

4.86 per cent because most of the villages falling under this block are within Aizawl Town (City, at present). At the same time, the number of beneficiaries was higher than the total number of households as per the preliminary (baseline) survey in East Lungdar RD Block. According to the record of the government and the observations of some researches, newly-formed households after the baseline survey and migration were the main reasons for the excessively high coverage percentage in this Block. Table 4.5 present the RD Block-Wise number of NLUP beneficiaries.

Table 4.5
Number of NLUP Beneficiaries in Mizoram: RD Block-Wise (1990-91 to 1996-97)

Sl. No.	*RD Blocks*	*Total No. of Households*	*No. of Beneficiaries (Households)*	*Percentage of Beneficiaries*
1.	Thingsulthliah	5806	3182	54.81
2.	West Phaileng	4685	3295	70.33
3.	Reiek	2549	1734	68.03
4.	East Lungdar	4619	5069	109.74
5.	Thingdawl	9572	6421	67.08
6.	Zawlnuam	8025	4073	50.75
7.	Serchhip	5569	4383	78.70
8.	Lungsen	5478	4696	85.72
9.	Tlangnuam	38385	1867	4.86
10.	Lunglei	10684	3064	28.68
11.	Khawzawl	11302	8712	77.08
12.	Ngopa	2757	2529	91.73
	TOTAL	**109431**	**49025**	**44.80**

Source: *Project Report of NLUP*, Commissionerate of Rural Development, Government of Mizoram, 1997 (Zoramchhana, 2000).

Although the original target of the programme was to cover the entire 20 RD blocks by the end of the Eighth Five Year Plan (i.e. 1997), only 12 were covered within the stipulated time frame. The number of beneficiaries under the scheme was still below expected even in the covered RD blocks. Inadequate funding from the centre was attributable to the slow progress of the programme (Zoramchhana, 2000). In spite of the state government's intention to continue to cover the entire state during the Ninth Plan period, the programme underwent a serious setback due to change in ministry. The Congress Ministry that had initiated the programme two times, in

1984 and in 1991, was replaced by Mizo National Front in the General Elections in 1998. Consequently, the remaining eight RD blocks could not be covered by the scheme.

4.5. Analysis of Sectoral Distribution of Beneficiaries

The sector-wise distribution of NLUP beneficiaries presented in Figure 4.1 shows the dominance of agriculture and allied sector, while the contribution of industrial sector is the lowest. The number of beneficiaries under agriculture and allied sector was 27469 which is 56 per cent of the total beneficiaries. At the same time, animal husbandry and veterinary sector having 27469 beneficiaries constituted 37 per cent, while the 3359 beneficiaries undertaking industrial activities constituted only seven per cent of the total beneficiaries. This sectoral distribution of beneficiaries is quite justifiable considering the poor communication infrastructures for the development of industrial and service sector in rural areas side by side with the existing state of agrarian economy.

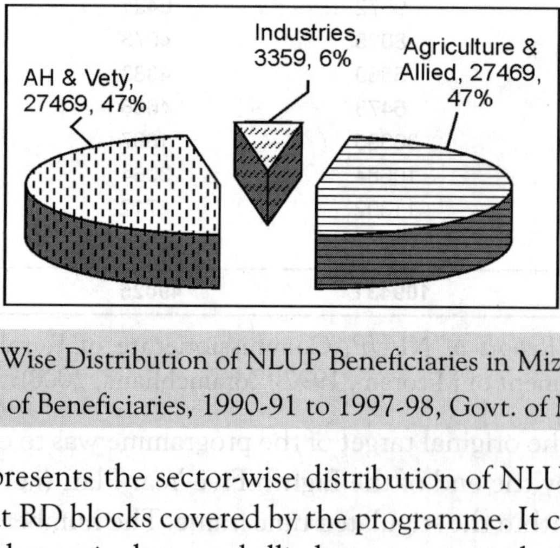

Fig. 4.1: Sector-Wise Distribution of NLUP Beneficiaries in Mizoram, 1991-97
Source: Abstract of Beneficiaries, 1990-91 to 1997-98, Govt. of Mizoram.

Table 4.6 presents the sector-wise distribution of NLUP beneficiaries among different RD blocks covered by the programme. It can be observed from this table that agriculture and allied sector occupied a dominant share in six blocks, namely Reiek, East Lungdar, Thingdawl, Zawlnuam, Serchhip, and Khawzawl, while the share of AH & Vety is higher than agriculture and allied in the RD blocks of Thingsulthliah, West Phaileng, Lungsen, Lunglei, and Ngopa. At the same time, the contribution of industrial sector is relatively low in most of the cases. It is highest in Thingsulthliah block

Table 4.6
Sector-Wise Distribution of Beneficiaries of NLUP (1991-97) in Different RD Blocks

Sl. No	RD Blocks	No. of Beneficiaries				Percentage of Beneficiaries			
		Agri. & Allied	AH & Vety	Industrial Sector	Total	Agri. & Allied	AH & Vety	Industrial Sector	Total
1.	Thingsulthliah	1423	1438	321	3182	44.72	45.19	10.09	100
2.	West Phaileng	1521	1626	148	3295	46.16	49.35	4.49	100
3.	Reiek	903	800	31	1734	52.08	46.14	1.79	100
4.	East Lungdar	3258	1472	339	5069	64.27	29.04	6.69	100
5.	Thingdawl	4715	1245	461	6421	73.43	19.39	7.18	100
6.	Zawlnuam	3055	885	163	4103	74.46	21.57	3.97	100
7.	Serchhip	2960	1023	401	4384	67.52	23.33	9.15	100
8.	Lungsen	2066	2308	322	4696	43.99	49.15	6.86	100
9.	Tlangnuam	853	852	102	1807	47.21	47.15	5.64	100
10.	Lunglei	1343	1438	283	3064	43.83	46.93	9.24	100
11.	Khawzawl	4810	3296	606	8712	55.21	37.83	6.96	100
12.	Ngopa	562	1887	180	2629	21.38	71.78	6.85	100
	TOTAL	**27469**	**18270**	**3357**	**49096**	**55.95**	**37.21**	**6.84**	**100**

Source: Abstract of NLUP Beneficiaries, Government of Mizoram, 1998 (Zoramchhana, 2000).

(10.9 per cent) and lowest in Reiek block (1.79 per cent). Since the programme focussed mainly on the jhumia families, the programme basically excluded the urban areas where land-based activities could not be undertaken. Accordingly, the minimal share of industrial sector could be mainly attributable to the exclusion of urban areas (especially Aizawl) under the scheme.

Table 4.7 presents the trade-wise distribution of the beneficiaries across the three sectors. The major trades under agriculture and allied sector are Tung cultivation (20.14 per cent, WRC (20.08 per cent), and orange cultivation (16.15 percent). These three major trades accounted for more than half (56.37 per cent) of the total number of beneficiaries under the sector. Other significant trades in terms of number of beneficiaries under agriculture and allied sector are Hatkora (7.57 per cent), Betelnut or Arecanut (6.42 per cent), Sugarcane (5.71 per cent), Pisciculture (5.29 per cent), Passion Fruit (4.48 per cent), and Horticulture (4.05 per cent). They accounted for 33.52 per cent of the beneficiaries under the sector. The appearance of horticulture as one of the trades is quite confusing as the term 'horticulture' is normally used to denote several plantation crops. However, it is believed that this trade (i.e. horticulture) was used to imply activities related to horticulture which could not be easily clubbed under any one of the stated specific trades. Thus, it can be concluded from Table 4.7 that around 90 per cent of the beneficiaries under agriculture and allied sector were accounted for by nine trades only.

Extreme majority of the beneficiaries under Animal Husbandry and Veterinary were found to be clustering in two trades which accounted for 71.08 per cent of the beneficiaries. The two major trades were Piggery (49.57 per cent) and Hill Cattle (30.51 per cent). Other trades under the sector with high number of beneficiaries were Dairy (5.79 per cent), Poultry (4.98 per cent), Goat Rearing (4.21 per cent), and Mithun (3.68 per cent). Thus, 89.74 per cent of the total beneficiaries under AH & Vety sector were in six major trades-piggery, hill cattle, dairy, poultry, goat rearing, and mithun.

It can also be observed from Table 4.7 that majority (64.01 per cent) of the NLUP beneficiaries undertaking industrial trades were in three trades, namely Carpentry (30.89 per cent), Tailoring (20.85 per cent) and Rice Miller (12.27 per cent). Other significant trades next to these major trades were Handloom (7.72 per cent), Bakery (6.40 per cent), Blacksmithy (4.65 per cent), and Shoe Repairing (3.40 per cent). These trades constituted 22.17 per cent of the beneficiaries under this sector. Thus, out of the 17 trades under industrial sector, only seven trades accounted for 86.18 per cent of the beneficiaries. One thing that is very clear from the pattern of the distribution of industrial trades was the dominance of activities based on local resources as well as local market. Thus, the success or failure of this sector would greatly depend upon the local market conditions. To sum up, more than two-thirds of the NLUP beneficiaries across the three sectors were in around 20 major activities or trades.

4.6. Assessment of NLUP (1991-97)

Having presented the operational procedures, expenditures, and distribution of beneficiaries on different trades, it was felt necessary to undertake an assessment of the implementation and impact of the programme. As almost 20 years had passed after the implementation of the scheme, it is not an easy task to undertake an in-depth analysis as it is not practicable to conduct fresh surveys among the beneficiaries. Since this is the case, it was decided to examine the impact of NLUP based on the secondary data (macro data)

Table 4.7
Distribution of NLUP Beneficiaries among the Three Major Sectors — Trade-Wise (1991-97)

Agriculture & Allied Sector			*AH &Vety Sector*		
Trade	*Beneficiaries*	*Percent*	*Trade*	*Beneficiaries*	*Percent*
WRC	5517	20.08	Hill Cattle	5574	30.51
Orange	4436	16.15	Dairying	1058	5.79
Lemon	193	0.70	Piggery	9057	49.57
Pineapple	484	1.76	Goat Rearing	769	4.21
Sugarcane	1569	5.71	Poultry	909	4.98
Hatkora	2079	7.57	Rabit Rearing	79	0.43
Terracing	771	2.81	Duck Rearing	63	0.34
Tung	5533	20.14	Sheep Rearing	88	0.48
Pisciculture	1454	5.29	Mithun	672	3.68
Valencia	44	0.16	Cross Breed	1	0.01
Mango	15	0.05	**TOTAL**	**18270**	**100**
Citronella	35	0.13	**Industrial Sector**		
Coffee	15	0.05	Arts & Painting	30	0.89
Tea	234	0.85	Bakery	215	6.40
Banana	405	1.47	Blacksmithy	156	4.65
Passion Fruit	1230	4.48	Cane & Bamboo	26	0.77
Sericulture	152	0.55	Carpentry	1037	30.89
Apple	77	0.28	Chow Making	52	1.55
Grape	16	0.06	Handloom	259	7.72
Jamir	18	0.07	Knitting	55	1.64
Kagzi lime	6	0.02	Motor Works	82	2.44
Teak	81	0.29	Radio Repairing	58	1.73
Coconut	68	0.25	Rice Miller	412	12.27
Betelvine	66	0.24	Shoe Repairing	114	3.40
Betelnut	1764	6.42	Steel Fabrication	14	0.42
Horticulutre	1112	4.05	Tailoring	700	20.85
Gardening	13	0.05	Tinsmithy	67	2.00
Squash (Chow Chow)	88	0.32	Watch Repairing	79	2.35
TOTAL	**27475**	**100**	Beauty Parlour	1	0.03
			TOTAL	**3357**	**100**

Source: *Abstract of NLUP Beneficiaries*, Government of Mizoram, 1998 (Zoramchhana, 2000).

obtained from various publications of the Statistical Handbook of Mizoram, published by Directorate of Economics and Statistics, Government of Mizoram. Similarly, assessment on the merits and drawbacks of the implementation of the programme was done based on various research findings and observations (published and unpublished). In spite of the limited availability of relevant information, the analysis is expected to serve a meaningful purpose for formulation of government policies in the future.

4.6.1. *Broad (Macro) Impacts*

To capture the impact of the NLUP in agricultural transformation and production, data on area under cultivation and production of major agriculture and allied crops in the pre- and post-project period were collected and presented in Table 4.8. The changes in the area and production were made with respect to the pre-NLUP period. Firstly, the total forest area increased from 1593500 hectares in 1990-91 to 1877500 hectares in 1998-99, which showed a 17.82 per cent increase during the period under comparison. As an increase in the geographical coverage of forest was one of the main objectives of NLUP, it can be concluded that there was significant

Table 4.8
Changes in the Area and Production of Major Agriculture and Allied Crops in Mizoram

A= Area in Hectares & P=Production in MT

Landuse Categories/Crops	1990-91*		1998-99**		Change (%)	
	A	P	A	P	A	P
Total Forest Area	1593500	—	1877500	—	17.82	—
Jhum (Paddy)	36716	35283	46634	59286	27.01	68.03
WRC	14607	28511	21758	51340	48.96	80.07
Maize	6640	11060	8681	16589	30.74	49.99
Ginger	2397	10495	7287	46648	204.01	344.48
Pulses	1341	1500	2374	3960	77.03	164.00
Oilseeds	1385	1600	7375	5682	432.49	255.13
Sugarcane	452	1792.00	952	6361	110.62	254.97
Orange	4559	13563.00	5482	32099	20.25	136.67
Banana	1914	8313.00	2484	35273	29.78	324.31
Pineapple	601	4249.00	898	2456	49.42	-42.20

Source: Various Issues of Statistical Handbook of Mizoram, Directorate Economics & Statistics., Government of Mizoram

** Due to unavailability of data (i) 2000-01 data is used for sugarcane, orange, banana, ginger, pulses and oilseeds; while 2003-04 data is used for Pineapple; and (ii) *Reference year for pulses and oilseeds is 1986-87, instead of 1990-91

increase in the forest cover in the state with the implementation of NLUP. This may be credited as a positive impact of the programme in achieving its objective.

Secondly, the table does not show reduction of jhum cultivation after the implementation of NLUP, rather it shows an increase by more than 68 per cent. The area under shifting cultivation increased from 36716 hectares in 1990-91 to 46634 hectares in 1998-99, while production also increased from 35283 to 59286 during the same period. The increase in the area and production of shifting cultivation is quite significant even after the population growth is taken into account. This is clearly an indication of the failure of the programme in containing or controlling the practice of shifting cultivation in Mizoram. Thirdly, the programme showed significant impact in increasing the area and production of WRC, which was set as one of the most important objectives of NLUP. Area and Production of WRC increased by 48.96 per cent and 68.03 per cent respectively. The positive change observed here are substantial enough to conclude that the programme significantly increased the area and production of WRC in Mizoram. Fourthly, with the exception of pineapple, all the other crops considered showed significant growth rates in terms of area and production. Even pineapple, which showed a negative growth of production, also recorded more than 49 per cent increase in cultivated area. Thus, it is safe to conclude that there were significant growth in areas and production of the major agricultural and horticultural crops in Mizoram after NLUP, while the area and production of shifting cultivation also recorded an increase as against targeted. At the same time, the achievement of the state in enlarging the forest cover is also quite commendable.

As AH & Vety sector accounted for about 37 per cent of the NLUP beneficiaries between 1991 and 1997, it may be worthwhile to study the changes in the livestock population in Mizoram so as to examine the impact of NLUP. Table 4.9 presents the change in the livestock population among the different blocks where NLUP was implemented between 1987 and 1997.

Table 4.9 shows that there was significant increase in the livestock population in Mizoram by more than 42 per cent between 1987 and 1997, as per the record of Quinquennial Livestock Census. Of the different RD Blocks covered by NLUP, Tlangnuam recorded the highest growth (158.8 per cent) followed by East Lungdar (90.3 per cent), while livestock population decreased in five blocks namely W. Phaileng, Serchhip, Lungsen,

Table 4.9
Changes in the Number of Livestock during 1987-97 in Mizoram

Block	*1987 (No. of animal)*			*1997 (No. of animal)*			*Change (%)*		
	Cattle	*Others*	*Total*	*Cattle*	*Others*	*Total*	*Cattle*	*Others*	*Total*
Thingsulthliah	1657	52176	53833	2092	73823	75915	26.3	41.5	41.0
W. Phaileng	846	104471	105317	728	68458	69186	-13.9	-34.5	-34.3
Reiek	715	29996	30711	1116	34942	36058	56.1	16.5	17.4
E. Lungdar	4269	73836	78105	2885	145750	148635	-32.4	97.4	90.3
Thingdawl	5256	71994	77250	2838	98645	101483	-46.0	37.0	31.4
Zawlnuam	1982	46622	48604	1270	80187	81457	-35.9	72.0	67.6
Serchhip	1218	42306	43524	812	75778	76590	-33.3	79.1	76.0
Lungsen	1532	33136	34668	507	26127	26634	-66.9	-21.2	-23.2
Tlangnuam	4749	92958	97707	3995	248843	252838	-15.9	167.7	158.8
Lunglei	2140	93692	95832	1374	83739	85113	-35.8	-10.6	-11.2
Khawzawl	6896	95624	102520	4315	137791	142106	-37.4	44.1	38.6
Ngopa	4114	57126	61240	2360	55591	57951	-42.6	-2.7	-5.4
TOTAL	**35374**	**793937**	**829311**	**24292**	**1129674**	**1153966**	**-31.3**	**42.3**	**39.1**

Source: 14th and 16th Quinquennial Livestock Census, 1987 and 1997, Government of Mizoram.

Lunglei, and Ngopa. The change in the livestock population was not in conformity with the distribution of NLUP beneficiaries undertaking AH & Vety trades as presented in Table 4.7. With the exception of Tlangnuam, the blocks that recorded negative growth were those where the NLUP beneficiaries under AH & Vety accounted for more than 40 per cent of the total number of beneficiaries. All these observations suggest the failure of the programme to increase livestock population in Mizoram. In other words, the NLUP under AH & Vety sector was not successful in bringing about an increase in production of livestock and its products.

4.6.2. *Observation of Some Studies*

In fact, it is very difficult to make a critical assessment of any programme after 10 years of its completion. With a change in the ministry in 1998, the Commissionerate of the Rural Development was reduced to a Directorate and most of the staff involved in the scheme were posted somewhere else and so they could not be easily identified for interview. The only method that appears to be practical for the study is to examine various research studies done during and immediately after the scheme was implemented. Accordingly, this section will attempt to examine the evaluation of the programme and its implementation as found in some research papers.

Firstly, the selection of beneficiaries was made by the concerned BDO based on the list of eligible families prepared in consultation with the VCs. The programme was to be restricted to those practising shifting cultivation and those below poverty line. However, the BDO was given discretionary power in the selection of beneficiaries (Maithani, 2005). There was also politicisation in the selection of beneficiaries; the really deserving families were often superseded by the better off families (Das, 2004). According to Das (2004) there was evidence of increasing involvement on the part of the political leaders in the selection of beneficiaries because it presents the opportunity to further their own party ends. The factor of affiliation with the ruling party seemed to have an important role in securing assistance under the scheme.

Secondly, the efficiency of the delivery system and monitoring was highly questionable. Singh (2007) observed that government services in extension and input supply were notoriously weak in small schemes with limited targets, let alone massive and highly centralised programmes such as the NLUP being executed on war footing. The bureaucracy was given overwhelming powers that override local village councils. Also, there is the question of management of funds in this heavily financed programme which had plenty of scope for leakages. A clear case of speculation on the use of funds exists in West Phaileng RD Block, where the number of beneficiaries exceeded the number of families enumerated in the 1991 Census by an astounding 45 per cent (Singh, 1996). In Thingsulthliah block, the total number of beneficiaries as recorded in the state headquarters was 4654, but the total number of beneficiaries observed when visited was 4400 (Das, 2004). Further, the monitoring system does not highlight the problems of implementation and the effectiveness of the programme (Garbyal, 1999).

Thirdly, there was an apparent lack of coordination among the government officials, the voluntary organisations, and the village councils (Das, 2004). Successful implementation of the programme requires a close relationship between these agencies. The failure to forge a close relationship resulted in a feeling of animosity on the part of the people towards the officials. A serious problem was that there was no effort to involve the village councils in the operation of NLUP. The VCs practically played the role of protection and management of land in their respective jurisdiction, as was done by the *chiefs*. The absence of VCs, which is the most effective grassroots institution, in the monitoring and land allotment under the programme was a serious lapse in design. By divesting the Village Council from any role in the new scheme, its enforcement power was considerably reduced. Therefore, even when people continued practising shifting cultivation albeit covertly in small groups, there was no mechanism to check and take action right on the spot (Maithani, 2005). Thus, NLUP operated in such a way as to dislocate the well-organised system of shifting cultivation. In the villages where jhumming had been banned, people continued the practice in small groups that showed lack of discipline and foresight of the village councils (Singh, 2007). In addition, though the programme had serious implication to change the existing land tenure system, no proper mechanism for settlement of land issues and protection of landholding came up. This could and had resulted in the emergence of rural land market where rich people from urban areas buy the land already allotted for NLUP from the poor beneficiaries, thereby making land issues more complicated in rural areas of Mizoram.

Fourthly, another major drawback of the programme was the absence of market support for the produce (Garbyal, 1999). While formulating the programme, the availability of necessary infrastructure was overlooked. Though the government had made considerable efforts to create food and fruit processing facilities, its performance was not very encouraging, and the units tended to run at low capacity and rarely made a profit (Singh, 2007). Even though one of the stated objectives is to provide marketing outlets for the produce from the NLUP programme, there was no mention of how it was to be done.

Fifthly, although the NLUP scheme was largely concentrated on agriculture and allied sector, the land use system especially agricultural land use, did not undergo much change during the implementation period, and the land use pattern still remains the same in comparison to the pre-implementation period. This was mainly due to topographical constraints (Zoramchhana, 2000). In addition, though the programme had envisioned to encourage afforestation, there was no detail in the programme as to how it would be undertaken. Neither a separate fund appears to have been earmarked for this, nor had the Forest Department been associated with this work (Das, 2004).

Lastly, a serious concern should be the mistrust of the state. According to Leblhuber and Vanlalhruaia (2012), there was tremendous cause for concern as the failure of the project would seriously erode the credibility of the government. As the role of the government increased, the community's role in the management of the environment is reduced. As people lose their responsibilities, they also began to lose confidence in their communities, and consequently, in their ability to safeguard the traditional ethical code and to regulate their customary laws. In this way, people became increasingly dependent on government management programmes. Given the weak delivery and monitoring system of the NLUP programme, it was difficult for the jhum cultivators to trust an administration that was yet to prove its credibility. Such distrust also arose from the historical trajectory of top-down development plans, which provided neither the incentive nor opportunity for growth. A serious challenge to the regional development of Mizoram was posed by the underlying mistrust felt by local population towards government agencies.

4.7. Concluding Observations

The programme of NLUP implemented from 1990-91 to 1996-97 was formulated as an improvement over the previously implemented schemes.

It was implemented in an integrated manner, and introduced composite schemes rather than a single scheme. To overcome long gestation problem, each principal trade was linked to a subsidiary so as to yield quick returns. There is no denying the fact that the NLUP significantly impacted the lives and livelihood of the rural households, especially those practising shifting cultivation. Change in the agricultural practices and land use could be observed from the significant increase in forest areas and WRC in the state. At the same time, there were increasing areas and production of non-jhum crops (mostly plantation crops) like sugarcane, banana, pineapple, orange, etc. when compared with the pre-project period. Since these were the main trades under NLUP, one can conclude that the programme had commendable success in many areas.

However, the programme failed to achieve its main objective of putting an end to the age-old practice of shifting cultivation. This is clearly shown by the substantial increase in area and production of shifting cultivation during the years under comparison. The same attempt of abolishing jhumming was made two times in 1984 and 1987 by the government through introduction of NLUP and Jhum Control Project, respectively. However, these initiatives including NLUP (1991-97) failed to deliver the desired objective of putting an end to shifting cultivation. The reason for this failure could be credited to the strong attachment that the people have on jhumming side by side with the topographical and infrastructural constraints. It would be more practicable to attempt a gradual shift of the jhumia families towards settled cultivation, rather than attempting to abandon it within a short period of time. Observations by researchers may be cited here. Jhumming should not be viewed as an evil practice, but as a practice that had evolved over centuries as a reflex to the difficult physiographic character of land that is not suited for settled agriculture (Garbyal, 1999). More fundamentally, jhumming is not simply a vocation and source of livelihood for the villagers; it is essentially, and more importantly, a way of life for them (Das, 2004). Some parts of Mizoram are reasonably well-equipped for market entry, but others still have a long way to go. For such areas, till the time is favourable for the transition, it would be sensible to have a strategy to enhance the existing system of cultivation, while at the same time preparing the people for the opportunity to change (Singh, 2007).

The inefficiency of the delivery and monitoring system was the major cause of failure in most of the cases. Though the programme was intended to be integrated and was area oriented, the involvement of various departments like Agriculture, Horticulture, Animal Husbandry, Industries, and Forest was negligible. At the same time, the office of the Block Development Officer was given high authority in the selection and finalisation of trades, without active participation of other stakeholders. This led the way for irregularities in the selection of beneficiaries (Das, 2004). One thing that becomes very clear at the outset is the wrong choice of stakeholders for the project. Neither the village councils nor the local NGOs and farmers' organisations were given stakes in the project implementation and monitoring. Their active participation is even more critical on issues of land use and management. The significance of the participation of the vibrant village institutions like VC and NGOs is the most essential factor for the success of any scheme.

5

MIZORAM INTODELHNA PROJECT
(PROJECT FOR SELF-SUFFICIENCY IN MIZORAM)

5.1. Introduction

The second round of NLUP initiated in 1991 again suffered a serious setback with the change in the ministry in the General Assembly Election of 1998. The programme was immediately discontinued with the coming of Mizo National Front (MNF) Government led by Zoramthanga. The new government initiated a new line of thinking for jhum control policy at the backdrop of the failure of previously implemented schemes. The MNF Party was the one that discontinued the NLUP started in 1984 and implemented its own scheme named Jhum Control Project (JCP) in 1987-88. However, with its defeat in the 1989 General Election, the JCP was immediately discontinued by the subsequent Congress Government which revived NLUP in 1991. Again back in power, the MNF in their endeavour for a major breakthrough in the development process considered it necessary to work out a development strategy aiming at efficient exploitation of local resources, increasing productivity, and to study the whole gamut of the causes of rural poverty, the shortcomings of the previous schemes, and to formulate a scheme for the development of the rural poor (Lianzela, 2008).

The new project so evolved was called the Mizoram Intodelhna Project (MIP) — *Project for Self-Sufficiency in Mizoram,* to be funded through the central plan schemes of Additional Central Assistance (ACA) and Normal Central Assistance (NCA). The main aim of MIP was the upliftment of the rural poor especially the shifting cultivators (Sinha, 2012). Its main concern was attainment of self-sufficiency, food security, and better livelihood for the cultivators as a whole. The concept of watershed management was utilised, giving importance to jhumias (Ralte, 2015).

Since the MIP was one of the major land use policies adopted in Mizoram to abolish the practice of shifting cultivation by giving permanent means of livelihood for the jhumias, this chapter intends to give an outline of the project. However, systematic and more conclusive analytical results could not be arrived at due to the unavailability of required data and information. Nevertheless, it is expected that the information presented here would be relevant for reference in further academic exercise, and will form a base for policy making by learning about the success and/or failure of previous programmes.

5.2. Main Objectives of the Programme

The main objective of the programme was the upliftment of the rural poor especially the shifting cultivators, with a clear long term goal of the elimination of the age old practice of shifting cultivation in Mizoram. Further, its main concern was the creation of self-sufficiency, food security, and better livelihood. The objectives of the programme are as follows:

(a) To propagate against shifting cultivation practices among the farming population, especially the jhumia community of the state.
(b) To encourage settled and permanent farming through commercialisation of agriculture, horticulture, etc.
(c) To facilitate farm productivity through need-based programming which would include provision for critical inputs, e.g. water harvesting, irrigation, project area connectivity, and land development activity, etc.
(d) To programme for a cluster-based crop production and to facilitate buy-back networking and processing points.
(e) To frame an action plan for optimal tapping of existing potential cash crops and horticulture crops e.g. passion fruit, grapes etc. through specially focussed programmes and public private partnership (PPP).
(f) To ensure that market is assured for each of the activities of the

project and that such market would address the supply needs within the state, as well as that of the national and international market demands.

(g) To provide for gap filling funds in the nature of direct financing of unmet needs and critical plan gaps through fund provision made under state plan, and by way of making provision as state's share to various centrally sponsored scheme sources etc., including credit-linked programme and schemes.

(h) To formulate vital policy-making wish list with a view to facilitate the outflow of products from the state.

5.3. Targeted Families

Similar to the other land use programmes previously implemented, like NLUP and Jhum Control Project, the programme also laid out the targeted families clearly. Families to be covered under MIP are bona fide Indian citizens who are permanent residents of the villages of Mizoram, and

1. families who earn their livelihood from agriculture and allied activities including animal husbandry, and
2. families whose members do not have regular works or employment even if they are not cultivators.

While making the target population, the beneficiaries were also entrusted with certain responsibilities. That is, the beneficiary of MIP should abide by the following clauses and should give in writing his/her agreement to do so:

1. They should not utilise any part or portion of the assistance for anything other than the purpose for which it is given.
2. Any kind of the assistance should not be handed over to another person except with the written permission of the appropriate authority.
3. Any asset, movable or immovable, created or procured through the assistance should not be sold or given to others without the permission of the appropriate authority.
4. Before the completion of the scheme under the MIP, the beneficiary

should not migrate from the village without prior permission of the government.

5.4. Authorities of the Programme

With the commencement of the programme, a Task Force consisting of experts from different fields and prominent citizens was constituted to study the whole gamut of the causes of rural poverty, the shortcomings of the previous schemes, and to formulate a scheme for the development of the rural poor. In fact, the Task Force was the body that conceptualised the programme and worked out its detailed framework.

The actual implementation of the scheme saw the formation of the State Level Apex Committee under the chairmanship of the Chief Minister. The Apex Committee comprised of Agriculture Minister, Chief Secretary, Secretary of Agriculture Department, and other members appointed by the government. The Committee was responsible for consideration and approval of the programme activities formulated for MIP. Under the Apex Committee were two sub-committees, viz. Marketing Committee, and Programme Evaluation and Monitoring Committee. Meanwhile, the MIP establishment functioned as a separate Cell within the Directorate of Agriculture, Government of Mizoram. The Cell was entrusted with the roles of administration and supervision of the programme.

5.5. Programme Modalities

The Guidelines of MIP stated that the programme would primarily be a think tank and programme formulator and would not be involved in the direct execution of projects and programme elements. However, it would outsource the work of implementation through the appropriate Line Departments with whom programme elements and action planning are to be drawn up. Thus, it mainly relied on the existing men, material, and management with the line department in the implementation and actual execution of the various programme activities and projects.

The core beneficiaries of the programme activities were the small and marginal farmers either organised through self help groups (SHG) or through crop grower associations. The groups were encouraged to voluntarily organise themselves into interest groups. As per the policy guidelines, fund for the whole village (cluster) would be given (in each phase) to the farmers' association of that village. The association would deposit the fund in the nearby bank which would then be released at the right time. This was done so as to attain grassroots participation in the programme.

One of the important aspects of the programme was prioritisation of crops and selection of the size of beneficiaries based on the available resources. The underlying idea of crop prioritisation was import substitution for crops that could be easily grown in the state. These crops were given priority in the MIP for immediate production. They include potato, onion, garlic, pulses, edible oil (mustard oil), soyabean, and maize, while passion fruits, red oil palm, grapes, papaya, and some medicinal plants were also included in the revised guidelines. Instead of cultivating them by everyone and everywhere, cluster approach was taken into consideration. To facilitate this initiative, a memorandum of understanding (MoU) was signed with some firms and organisations for selected products like Oil Palm.

The MIP Guidelines also clearly specified how community organisation and institutional arrangement would be made available for the implementation and monitoring of the project activities. The monitoring activities were to be carried out through assigned programme functionaries. The task of data collection was to be outsourced to a reliable community based organisation (CBO). In addition, the task of independent and comprehensive evaluation was also to be outsourced. As per the record of the Agriculture Department, Mr. J.P. Jaiswal was engaged as consultant for evaluation of the programme and was paid Rs. 8.67 lakh as consultancy fee.

Recognising the significance of a well organised marketing system for the sustainability of the programme, the MIP also made marketing plan without earmarking fund for its execution (Lianzela, 2008). It was expected that the funds earmarked by the Government of India for development of agricultural marketing infrastructure would be made available for the development of such. Marketing Plan of MIP was so designed to enable MIP Marketing Board to avail all structural, technical, and financial assistance available under the scheme of National Horticulture Board, Agriculture Products Export Development Agency (APEDA), etc. MIP Marketing Board would act as the pioneering agency in the marketing and progressively take up action institutionalising the whole market system by creating market committees, market areas, market yards, sub-market yards, etc. Infrastructures such as warehouses, cold storages, buildings, and other structures for post-harvest processes in the market yards were to be constructed. Apart from agricultural produce, inputs required by the farmers would be made available in these markets.

5.6. Progress of the Implementation

Although evolved in 2001, the actual work of MIP started in 2002 under the supervision of the MIP Task Force. Each beneficiary, before getting the assistance, was required to prepare a project with the help of an expert in the field. Originally, the quantum of assistance proposed to the beneficiary was Rs. 50,000 and any amount above this would be met by the beneficiary himself (Lianzela, 2008). The fund was to be released in a phase manner. An amount of Rs. 7,500 per beneficiary would be released in the first year, and Rs. 15,000 and Rs. 12,500 were to be released in the second and third year respectively. However, the actual implementation showed that the beneficiaries were given only Rs. 11,500 in two instalments indicating a shortfall of 77 per cent from the original target amount.

Table 5.1 presents the number of beneficiaries and total amount of assistance provided in eight districts for the First and Second Phases of MIP. An amount of Rs. 7,500 per family was given to 30393 families with a total expenditure of Rs. 2279.475 lakh in the first phase, while Rs. 4,000 per family was given for 19314 families with a total expenditure of Rs. 772.56 lakh in all districts in the second phase. Thus, according to the available sources, a total of 49707 families were given assistance of Rs. 11,500 each and the total expenditure for beneficiary assistance under MIP amounted to Rs. 3052.035 lakh only (Rs. 30.52 crore). The reason for the reduction of assistance amount from the targeted Rs. 15,000 to Rs. 4,000 and its stoppage for the third instalment could not be clearly ascertained. However, the most probable reason is fund limitation. Though it was targeted to continue the aid to these families, there was a stop-gap due to the revealing and revising of the MIP guidelines (Ralte, 2015).

In addition to the cash assistance to the beneficiaries, other activities that were considered related to and facilitating the success of the programme were taken up. These activities can be grouped into eight sub-heads and is presented in Table 5.2. The expenditures were mostly made for the purpose of administration, institutional arrangements, and provision of necessary infrastructures. Of the total expenditure of Rs. 498.64 lakh, 30.17 per cent was made for administrative expenditures, including consultancy fee for

Table 5.1
Number of Families Assisted and Amount Disbursed under MIP in Mizoram

District	Phase-I (2002-03)			Phase-II (2002-03)			Phase-I & II Total	
	No. of Families	Amount (Rs. in Lakhs)	Amount per Family (Rs.)	No. of Families	Amount (Rs. In Lakhs)	Amount per Family (Rs)	No. of Families	Amount (Rs. In Lakhs)
Aizawl	7943	595.725	7500	4571	182.84	4000	12514	778.565
Lunglei	4509	338.175	7500	2076	83.04	4000	6585	421.215
Saiha	1564	117.3	7500	440	17.6	4000	2004	134.9
Kolasib	3025	226.875	7500	4254	170.16	4000	7279	397.035
Champhai	5664	424.8	7500	4028	161.12	4000	9692	585.92
Lawngtlai	727	54.525	7500	623	24.92	4000	1350	79.445
Mamit	3112	233.4	7500	1329	53.16	4000	4441	286.56
Serchhip	3849	288.675	7500	1993	79.72	4000	5842	368.395
Total	**30393**	**2279.475**	**7500**	**19314**	**772.56**	**4000**	**49707**	**3052.035**

Source: Lianzela (2008)

monitoring and evaluation. At the same time, assistance and facilitation of farmers' organisation (16.64 per cent), promotion of oil palm cultivation (12.03 per cent) and construction of link road (10.93 per cent) were other major expenditure heads.

Table 5.2
Expenditure on Various Activities Other than Beneficiary Assistances under MIP

Sl. No.	*Major Heads of Expenditure*	*Amount (Rs. in lakhs)*	*Percent*
1.	Administrative Expenses	150.45	30.17
2.	Assistance & Facilitation of Farmers Association	82.95	16.64
3.	Construction of Link Road	54.50	10.93
4.	Land Development	40.00	8.02
5.	Seeds Supply	47.17	9.46
6.	Material Supply	46.92	9.41
7.	Oil Palm Cultivation	60.00	12.03
8.	Establishment of Storage and Processing Unit	16.65	3.34
	TOTAL	**498.64**	**100**

Source: Laltanpuii Ralte (2015), *IJMSS*, Vol. 3 (8). pp.10-27.

Some of the major activities presented in Table 5.2 may be outlined here. Farm link roads from piggery village at Sairang to Sairum, from Tuitun to Pachhiat (Khamrang) and Kawrthingdeng Zau to Rangvamual were constructed at the costs of Rs. 27 lakh, Rs. 27 lakh and Rs. 50,000 respectively under the MIP. An expenditure of Rs. 40 lakh was spent for development of 45 hectares of WRC area at Saihapui Village using machineries. Though not reflected in Table 5.2, construction of Multipurpose Cold Storage Unit with a total cost of Rs. 500 lakh at Vairengte through NABARD loans in 2006 may also be mentioned here as it was within the policy framework of MIP. Fibre Extraction machine for extraction of pineapple fibre was purchased at a cost of Rs. 9.83 lakh and Chicken Hatchery Unit was also established at an expenditure of Rs. 3.78 lakh. An amount of Rs. 25.20 lakh was spent for the office expenses of the various farmers associations formed under the programme. A number of families at Champhai and its vicinity who grew passion fruit were given GI Wire worth Rs. 45.86 lakh, while cultivators of hatkora in Sairang, Khamrang, and Kawnpui villages were supplied saplings and seeds costing Rs. 9.39 lakh.

Moreover, 6 lakh stevia seedlings were imported from Pune at an expenditure of Rs. 30.35 lakh for distribution to 20 families of Kolasib and Aizawl districts. An intensive measure was taken for the cultivation of Red Oil Palm and a total expenditure of Rs. 30 lakh was spent on it.

5.7. Notes of Evaluation

Prior to the implementation of MIP, land use projects like NLUP and Jhum Control were implemented in Mizoram with an aim to do away the traditional practice of shifting cultivation. As noted in the previous chapters, the initiatives did not show clear and impressive success due to various reasons. The MIP was evolved as an improved one with more or less similar objectives taking into account the lacunae of the previous programmes, thereby, having better chance of success. The emphasis on group approach in MIP, rather than beneficiary followed under NLUP (1991-97), was quite attractive and invited better participation in implementation and monitoring. It is understood that a participatory project is likely to be a success. Further, the underlying principle on the nature and roles of the MIP Task Force to be a '*think-thank*' for gap analysis and channelising of available funds for projects with higher scope of success was also a welcomed initiative.

One of the positive signals implicating the success of MIP can be found in Oil Palm Cultivation. This was undertaken in the form of contract farming for seeds supply as well as buy-back agreements with companies from outside the state. To encourage its success in the long run, the Mizoram Oil Palm (Regulation of Production and Processing) Act, 2004 was enacted. Cultivation of oil palm is continued till today, and with its adoption as one of the trades under NLUP (2011), more and more families have entered into its venture. A number of families, especially from Kolasib and Mamit districts, have earned substantial income from the sale of oil palm produce.

However, the actual implementation of MIP showed significant deviation from its objectives and principles, as set out in the Policy Guidelines, in many respects. *Firstly*, the serious challenge to MIP was fund constraint. The entire fund allocation was less than Rs. 50 crore which was considered too small an amount to make much headway. Also, involvement of line departments was minimal and frequent changes of programmes and guidelines created confusion (JICA Study, 2014). In respect to the beneficiary assistance, out of the total target of Rs. 50,000 per beneficiary, only Rs. 11,500 could be delivered in two instalments. This is only 23 per cent (a shortfall of 77 per cent) of the target amount, which clearly denotes the failure of the programme. The assistance amount that could be delivered was too meagre to have significant impact for changes in the livelihood activities of the family, especially for complete abandonment of shifting cultivation in rural areas. *Secondly*, the crucial point for the success of any scheme would be the selection of beneficiaries. The policy guidelines of MIP did not clearly establish the mechanism for identification of clusters, selection of beneficiaries, and the methodology for selecting particular crops. It rather looked like a simple selection of families and giving cash assistance without much care about the purpose and activities to be undertaken. There was no systematic procedure for allocation of particular crops to the selected beneficiaries, and there was no report regarding the classification of beneficiaries among the different trades (crops) either.

Thirdly, absence of strict monitoring and evaluation should be another area of concern. A Sub-Committee for Monitoring and Evaluation was constituted by the State Government in 2004; however, there was no concrete and tangible initiative for its materialisation. Further, a sum of Rs. 8.67 lakh was spent as consultancy fee for evaluation done by J.P. Jaiswal. However, it is not known to the public whether the report and suggestions made by the consultant were endorsed and accommodated in the subsequent years. *Fourthly*, import of foreign variety seeds of stevia by spending huge amount did not have results in the subsequent years as there is no record, official or otherwise, on the production of stevia in the state till date. *Fifthly*, the failure of the marketing facilitation projects under MIP could be gauged from the poor performance of plants and machineries installed under it. Fibre Extraction machine, Gas Fired Dryer Trolley, Chicken Hatchery Unit, Ginger Pack House, Cold Storage, etc. set up under the funding of MIP were inoperative immediately after they were established. Absence of an effective Operation and Maintenance (OM) framework for these infrastructures could be attributed to their failure.

Lastly, poor delivery of the assistance whether in cash or kind (in addition to the inability to provide full assistance as targeted) was a serious setback of the programme. Out of the 1239 piglets distributed by the Rural Development Department at Lunglei and Hnahthial RD blocks under the MIP, it was found that only eight survived. These piglets were purchased by the Government at the rate of Rs. 2,500 per piglet. The death rate was 94.46 per cent which means that the Government incurred a loss of Rs. 30 lakh. Moreover, triple the price of each piglet was spent for transporting them from Shillong to the distribution points. These piglets were said to be of superior breed and were professed to have been examined by veterinarians before distribution. With such types of implementation of the programmes meant for the development of the farmers, the very notion of development was very difficult to achieve (Ralte, 2015).

Like the previous land use programmes, the MIP also had a serious setback with the defeat of the MNF party in the General Assembly Election in 2008. The Congress Party which came into ministry discontinued the programme and reinstalled New Land Use Policy in a more comprehensive way.

6

COMPREHENSIVE NEW LAND USE POLICY, 2011

AN OUTLINE OF THE IMPLEMENTATION FRAMEWORK

6.1. Introduction

Mizoram has experienced several initiatives to attain sustainable land utilisation that aims at moving the population away from the age-old practice of shifting cultivation (jhumming) to one that is permanent, remunerative, and sustainable. Several ministries under different political parties ushered in their own initiatives. All major political parties under different leaderships had their own concepts for land use policy that were implemented once they came into office. The People Conference (PC) Party, now rechristened Mizoram People Conference (MPC), under the leadership of Brig T. Sailo initiated a project called 'Garden Colony' in 1978; and the Mizo National Front (MNF) Government led by Laldenga implemented 'Jhum Control Policy' in 1987 and the same party under the leadership of Zoramthanga implemented 'Mizoram Intodelhna Project' (Project for Self-sufficiency in Mizoram) in 2002. The Indian National Congress (INC) under the leadership of Lal Thanhawla implemented New Land Use Policy (NLUP) in 1984 and in 1990-91. After a gap of 10 years, immediately after General Election 2008, the INC revived in an endeavour to implement NLUP in a more comprehensive way. Several commentators attributed the landslide victory of INC in the 2008 Election to its propaganda of implementing the policy in an improved form, in terms of coverage and amount of assistances.

At the same time, the people had endeavoured to undertake sustainable land use and move away from the traditional practice of shifting cultivation to that of permanent cultivation.

With a view of the grave economic deprivation of the common people, especially the farmers who constitute about 70 per cent of the total population of Mizoram, the NLUP that was conceived and implemented in 1984 in a small scale and later in an improved form in 1992, was again implemented in 2011 in a larger scale after the Congress Party came into power in 2008. Further modifications and better frameworks were made to the policy following the suggestions of Government of India that envisaged a five year period for the project to be completed with a cost of staggering Rs. 2,800 crore (Thangliana, 2013). Although the groundwork was initiated in 2009, the NLUP was officially launched on 14 January 2011.This particular day is now celebrated as 'Farmers' Day' (*Kuthnathawktute Ni*, in Mizo). The programme encompasses a wide range of activities and a total of 1.2 lakh families were targeted to be covered.

6.2. Objectives and Target Groups

The NLUP (2011) is a versatile and encompassing mechanism for stable economy, environment protection, land reforms, and reclamation. The main aim of the NLUP is to develop and give all the farmers in the state suitable, permanent, and stable means of livelihood. The aims and objectives as given in the Policy Manual 2009 are as follows:

1. To put an end to wasteful shifting cultivation.
2. To ensure that all farmers have land of their own so that they can pursue permanent means of livelihood under agriculture (and allied), industry, or animal husbandry sectors.
3. To develop all the lands suitable for wet rice cultivation so as to attain self-sufficiency in rice and vegetables.
4. To re-afforest the land and conserve those allocated to the NLUP beneficiaries so as to regenerate the ecosystem. This will help stabilise the climatic changes wrought by global warming, rejuvenate the flora and fauna, and make Mizoram a better place to live in.
5. To set up marketing infrastructure so that the successful farmers

and beneficiaries under NLUP can have viable commercial outlets for their products.

Like the previous land use programmes, the NLUP also clearly identified the target groups to be covered. Persons having stable and permanent means of livelihood, and permanent employees of the government and other organised bodies were excluded from availing the benefits. The target groups presented in the policy guidelines are as follows:

1. Permanent inhabitants of Mizoram who are bona fide Indian citizens.
2. Families who eke out subsistence livelihood from jhumming.
3. Families with no permanent trade for their livelihood, even if they are not dependent on jhumming.
4. Only those families who have set up independent households at least for one year will be eligible for assistance under NLUP, other conditions remaining the same.
5. Ongoing projects undertaken individually or as a group under Centrally Sponsored Scheme (CSS) that are deemed economically viable may be continued under NLUP as convergence or gap-filling measures.

Further eligibility criteria were added by making amendments to the policy guidelines in 2011, which set the ceiling on the annual income of the families as follows: (i) for families living in the urban areas, not exceeding Rs. 1,00,000, and (ii) for families living in the rural areas, not exceeding Rs. 50,000.

The beneficiaries were to always keep in mind that the assistances are to be utilised only for the purpose it is granted. They should have an undertaking signed to give their best for the success of the scheme, and there were clear provisions for punishment of misuse of the assistances. The beneficiaries were expected to keep the following points in mind:

1. The assistance is not to be used for any other purpose except for the purpose of which it is granted.
2. The assistances received in kind are not to be sold or gifted to others without the permission of the government.
3. The trade/activity under the scheme, whether fully or partially

developed, is not to be sold or transferred to others without the permission of the government. However, this does not include the by-products of the trade/activity.

4. Without prior permission of the government, no beneficiary should migrate before completing their trade/activity.

6.3. Funding Pattern of NLUP

The groundwork for the implementation commenced in the beginning of 2009 when the government of Mizoram constituted the top authority for NLUP — an Apex Board chaired by the Chief Minister. In addition, the NLUP Implementing Board (NIB) was established under the Apex Board to serve as the executive agency of the project. The NIB is a Government society endowed with wide ranging financial autonomy. It was instituted solely for the purpose of the NLUP project and is in direct contact with the participating Government departments. Right from its inception, the NIB worked hard in preparing a Detailed Project Report (DPR) and the financial requirement for it was met from plan budget allocation of the State Government. The DPR of NLUP amounting to Rs. 2,526.98 crore, excluding beneficiary contribution, was submitted to the Planning Commission on 19.6.2009. After a number of deliberations at various levels of the Central Government, the Cabinet Committee on Economic Affairs (CCEA) chaired by the Prime Minister approved a total outlay of Rs. 2,873.13 crore on the 2 July 2010 for the NLUP project for five years starting from the financial year of 2010-11.

An abstract of the funding pattern for NLUP as approved by CCEA is presented in Table 6.1. It is broadly divided into three components: *management component* for administration and direction of the project, *development component* for beneficiary assistance in cash or kind, and *infrastructure component* for creation of supporting infrastructure to facilitate the success and sustainability of the programme. Component-wise share in the total expenditure as observed in this table shows the dominance of the development component (56.39 per cent) followed by infrastructure component (41.1 per cent) and management component (2.51 per cent).

There were four sources of funding, viz. CSS/Central Shares (34.83 per cent), Additional Central Assistance (ACA) (12.34 per cent), Additional Subsidy for beneficiary through ACA (50.60 per cent), and Beneficiary Contribution (12.05 per cent). The beneficiaries were not

Table 6.1
Abstract of Funding Pattern for NLUP as approved by CCEA

Component	*CSS/ Central Share*	*ACA (State Share through the ACA and outright ACA)*	*Additional Subsidy through ACA for beneficiary*	*Total ACA/SPA (3+4)*	*Beneficiary Contribution*	*Total Cost*
(1)	(2)	(3)	(4)	(5)	(6)	(7)
Management	—	72.20	—	72.20	—	72.20
Development	110.34	—	1171.66	1171.66	338.15	1620.15
Infrastructure	890.50	282.28	282.28	282.28	8.00	1180.78
Total	**1000.84**	**354.48**	**1453.94**	**1526.14**	**346.15**	**2873.13**

Source: Draft Annual Plan—New Land Use Policy 2013-14, Government of Mizoram

expected to give their contribution in cash, but in the form of physical labour that would be inputted by them to make their activity a success. The table shows that the two categories of ACA were the main funding sources that contributed 62.94 per cent of the total expenditure. More than 72.32 per cent of the development component (mainly for beneficiary assistances) was from beneficiary subsidy through ACA, while the remaining 27.68 per cent was from CSS/Central shares, especially meant for material supply. Further, the main chunk of infrastructure component was to be obtained from CSS, which constitutes 75.42 per cent.

One crucial objective of NLUP is the convergence of the ongoing Central Sponsored Schemes with NLUP so as to avoid duplication of works by two or more different departments. This is called *Convergence Scheme*. The experience of the state government showed that several CSS meant for construction of necessary infrastructure undertaken by different departments like Rural Development, Agriculture, Forest, etc. were implemented by the departments in their own way without much consideration of what was being done by the others. This creates the possibility of duplication of work, and thus, pooling all these funds towards common goals and objectives would have significant results. This was the idea behind the creation of NLUP Convergence Scheme. The scheme-wise convergence plan for NLUP as approved by CCEA is presented in Table 6.2.

The table indicates that infrastructure development is the basic objective of this convergence scheme as the total allocation towards it

Table 6.2
Allocation to be made from CSS/Central Share under Convergence Scheme for NLUP as approved by CCEA

Sl. No.	Sector/ Heads	CSS/Central Share (Rs. Crores)	Component	Sources (Name of Centrally Sponsored Schemes)
1.	Agriculture	12.90	Development	ISOPOM
2.	Horticulture	52.99	- do -	TM & NMMP
3.	Fishery	15.00	- do -	Not Specified
4.	S&WC	12.00	- do -	Rubber Board & Coffee Board
5.	Forest	17.45	- do -	NBM
6.	Rural Godown	27.90	Infrastructure	BRGF & ACA
7.	Water Harvesting	87.05	- do -	MGNREGA
8.	Agri. Link Road	772.60	- do -	MGNREGA
9.	Ice Plant, etc	0.32	- do -	NFDB
10.	Hydrogers	2.63	- do -	MNRE
	Total	**1000.84**		

Source: CCEA Note, May 2010 vide M-13015/18/Mizo/2008-09/SP-NE, Planning Commission, Government of India

Note: (1) ISOPOM: Integrated Scheme of Oilseeds, Pulses, Oil Palm and Maize, (2) TM: Technology Mission, (3) NMMP: National Mission on Medicinal Plants, (4) NBM: National Bamboo Mission, (5) BRGF: Backward Region Grant Fund, (6) ACA: Additional Central Assistance, (7) MGNREGA: Mahatma Gandhi National Rural Employment Guarantee Act, (8) NFDB: National Fisheries Development Board, and (9) MNRE: Ministry of New and Renewable Energy

constituted 88.98 per cent, while developmental expenditure constituted only 11.02 per cent. The development component to be met from convergence scheme was normally meant for seeds/material supplies. Agriculture link road, to be converged with MGNREGA under Rural Development (RD) Department, was the most significant source of CSS which contributed more than 77 per cent of the total allocation under the convergence scheme. In fact, unfavourable hill terrain remains to be the main hurdle for agriculture development, especially for marketing. So, more fund allocation on it is justified. Water Harvesting Scheme from MGNREGA was another major contributor of infrastructure development by constituting about nine per cent. Scheme-wise contribution also shows the dominance of MGNREGA having 85.89 per cent contribution which is followed by horticulture schemes of Technology Mission (TM) and National Mission on Medicinal Plants (NMMP) with total estimated contribution of Rs. 52.99 crore (5.29 per cent).

6.4. Financial and Physical Targets for Various Activities

Beneficiaries of NLUP were given a wide range of choice in the selection of trades to be undertaken under the programme. There were 59 major activities, called *trades*, distributed over nine sectors under separate government departments, called *Line Departments*. Initially, there were eight sectors, but with the entry of Urban Development & Poverty Alleviation (UD&PA) in 2013-14, the task of implementing 10 industrial trades in Aizawl City were transferred to UD & PA. However, the same trades under this department would still be under Industries Department in areas other than Aizawl. Names of the trades and sector wise allocation of the number of trades are presented in Table 6.3. Unlike the NLUP implemented before in 1984 and 1991, the 2011 scheme did not have *subsidiary trades* to supplement the requirements of the beneficiaries before the start of production.

Of the nine sectors, industrial sector had the highest number of trades, which would be even higher if the various activities under small and micro-enterprises are taken into account. There were two sectors (departments) which have only one trade, namely, forest and sericulture. Among the land based sector, Horticulture Department accommodated the highest number of trades. It may be noted that the programme was implemented in a comprehensive way by also covering the urban poor who do not possess land for undertaking land based activities. Accordingly, all such urban families were attempted to be put under industrial sector, thus significantly inflating the number of trades and beneficiaries under this sector. Further, consideration had to be made for some urban poor who do not possess the necessary skills and space to implement any of the notified trades. They were given lower amount of cash assistance but were free to take up any economic activity suitable to them using the assistance. The activities that could not be easily classified under specific trades were clubbed under *small and micro-enterprises (S&ME)*.

Targets for beneficiary assistance, whether in cash or kind, were made separately for all trades. This was done to fulfil all the requirements, at

Table 6.3
NLUP Trades under different Line Departments

Sl. No.	Sector/Line Departments	No. of Trades	Name of Trades			
1.	Agriculture	4	WRC-I	WRC-II	Oil Palm	Sugarcane
2.	Horticulture	9	Passion Fruit	Grapes	M. Orange	Pineapple
			Aloe Vera	Arecanut	Tung	Tea
			Squash (Chayote)			
3.	AH &Vety	4	Dairy Farming	Poultry	Piggery	Hill Cattle/Mithun
4.	S&WC	3	Coffee	Rubber	Brooms	
5.	Fisheries	2	Aquaculture	Polyculture		
6.	Forest	1	Bamboo			
7.	Sericulture	1	Mulberry			
8.	Industries	25	Auto Rickshaw	Automobile works	Cane & Bamboo Making	Leather & Hood Works
			Bakery	Beauty Parlour	Black Smithy	Broom Making
			Carpentry-I	Carpentry-II	Chow Making	DTP
			Electronic Repair	Hair Cutting	Handloom	Knitting
			Petty Trade-I	Petty Trade-IV	Photography	Rice Hulling
			Agarbati	Steel Fabrication	Tailoring	Tinsmithy
			Small & Micro-enterprises			
9.	UD & PA	10	Automobile	Beauty Parlour	DTP	Electronic Repairing
			Hair Cutting	Knitting	Photo	Tailoring
			Shoe Repairing	Leather & Hood Works		
	Total	**59**				

Source: NLUP Implementing Board, Government of Mizoram, 2016.

least at the minimum level, for the successful completion of the trades. It was Rs. 1 lakh on an average for trades, while some industrial activities or micro-enterprises under Industries and UD & PA departments were below this amount. The range of the value of assistances (financial and material) for all sectors is presented in Table 6.4. It may be noted that assistance for some trades under Agriculture, Horticulture, AH & Vety and Industries exceeded the average target of Rs. 1 lakh. This is basically due to the requirement for the completion of the delivery and functioning of the material assistances. For example, auto-rickshaw under Industries costs around Rs. 1 lakh. To make the vehicle functional for the beneficiaries, certain requirements like registration fee, insurance, etc. has to be met. Therefore, the amount of assistance increased in such cases.

Table 6.4
Range of Financial and Material Assistances under NLUP

Sl. No.	*Sector/Department*	*Trades*	*Range of Assistance (Rs)*
1.	Agriculture	4	1,00,000 – 1,20,000
2.	Horticulture	9	1,00,000 – 1,20,000
3.	Animal Husbandry & Veterinary	4	1,00,000 – 1,25,000
4.	Soil & Water Conservation	3	80,000 – 1,00,000
5.	Fisheries	2	1,00,000
6.	Environment & Forest	1	1,00,000
7.	Sericulture	1	1,00,000
8.	Industries	25	50,000 – 1,16,000
9.	Urban Development & Poverty Alleviation	10	50,000 – 1,00,000

Source: NABCONS, *Mid-Term Assessment of NLUP*, 2013

The programme set a target of 1,20,000 families to be covered within a span of five years starting from 2010-11. The total target was based on the results of 'Baseline Survey' conducted by Central Young Mizo Association (CYMA) through its local branches in 2009. Physical target was then made separately for each economic sector by taking into consideration the data of the Economic Classification of the Population in 1991 Population Census, and the availability of arable land for different agriculture and allied activities. Table 6.5 presents the sector-wise distribution of physical target (number of families) over a period of five years. The largest number of beneficiaries were projected to adopt trades under agriculture sector (26.33

per cent) followed by horticulture (24 per cent) and only 5.42 per cent of the total beneficiaries were targeted to adopt the industrial trades.

Table 6.5
Sector-Wise Physical Targets to be covered under NLUP in Five Years

Sector	2010-11	2011-12	2012-13	2013-14	2014-15	Total	Percent
Agriculture	12340	4815	4815	4815	4815	31600	26.33
Horticulture	11520	4320	4320	4320	4320	28800	24.00
Sericulture	2500	1500	1500	1500	1500	8500	7.08
Fishery	1200	450	450	450	450	3000	2.50
Soil & Water Conservation	4000	1100	1100	1100	1100	8400	7.00
AH &Vety	5200	3415	3415	3415	3415	18860	15.72
Industry	3200	825	825	825	825	6500	5.42
Forest	5179	1390	1390	1390	1391	10740	8.95
Others not specified	–	–	–	–	–	3600	3.00
Total	**45139**	**17815**	**17815**	**17815**	**17816**	**120000**	**100**

Source: Detailed Project Report of NLUP, Government of Mizoram, 2009.

A closer look at Table 6.5 shows that agriculture and allied sector was given due weightage in the allotment of physical targets. This is justified in consideration of the objectives and target groups of NLUP given in the policy guidelines, and because of the occupational distribution of the people where more than half of the population depends on agriculture and allied activities. Agriculture and allied sectors like agriculture, horticulture, sericulture, fishery, and soil and water conservation (S&WC) contributed 66.92 per cent of the total physical target, which would be 82.63 per cent if veterinary and animal husbandry (AH & Vety) is included. And since forest contributed 8.95 per cent, the total share of all land based sectors turned out to be 91.58 per cent of the total physical target. The target for industries (and micro-enterprises) sector having potential for generating employment and income both in urban and rural areas was only 5.42 per cent. Relatively lower number was earmarked for this sector as success of this sector largely depends on selection of beneficiaries and allocation of suitable activities that require skill and training, and also by considering the scenario that local industrial products are mainly driven by local demand, which can saturate with the entry of more people.

6.5. Organisational Structures of Project Management

The project has a four tier management system at the state, district, and village level for implementation, monitoring, and review of the programme. Their roles and duties are clearly specified in the policy manuals. A brief outline of the roles and responsibilities of these bodies may be discussed here. There is a high power committee at the State level called NLUP Apex Board headed by the Chief Minister and the Council of Ministers, Commissioners/Secretaries of concerned Line Departments and Expert/ Prominent Citizens as its members. The Apex Board is the policy-making authority with power to approve plan programme, allotment of funds, and overall supervision of the implementation of the programme.

Next to the Apex Board is the NLUP Implementing Board (NIB) with the Vice Chairman of the Apex Board as its Chairman. Members of the NIB are the heads of concerned line departments, experts, prominent citizens, and representatives of NGOs. The NIB is the executive body of the programme. It prepares the annual budget, makes guidelines relating to financial matters, projects and schemes and submits it to the Apex Board for approval. It helps the monitoring work of the programme by running a separate Monitoring Cell. It also takes necessary initiatives for formulation and implementation of marketing policies and has a Marketing Cell under it.

The third tier of the project management is the District Level NLUP Implementing Committee under the Chairmanship of Deputy Commissioners (DC) with district officers of the concerned departments, farmers, and NGOs as its members. The District Committee is entrusted with the responsibility of supervising and monitoring the implementation of the project, and to organise trainings and demonstrations if needed. The fourth tier is the Village Level NLUP Implementing Committee headed by President of the Village Council (VC) and all members of the Village Council, and prominent citizens appointed by NIB as its members. It is the responsibility of the village committee to maintain accounts and cash books, and collect required data for monitoring and progress review. It is to assist the district committees whenever required.

Meanwhile, the actual implementing agency of NLUP programmes of the different sectors are the respective departments — *Line Departments.* All related programmes are to be implemented by the concerned Line

Departments of the state government through the designated boards and committees at the various levels of administration given above. Funds earmarked for such programmes are allotted to line departments for release of required funds through the District Implementing Committee as per the requirements decided by the District Committee in consultation with Village Level Implementing Committee. The organisational structure of NLUP is presented in the form of a chart in Figure 6.1.

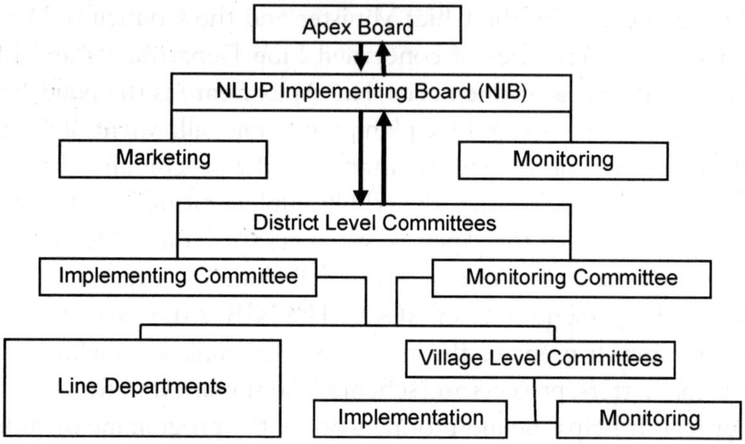

Fig. 6.1: Organisational Chart of Project Management

6.6. Selection of Beneficiaries and Allocation of Trades

The critical point for the success of massive schemes like NLUP is the selection of beneficiaries and allotment of trades based on their skills, experience, and commitments. Due care was taken to ensure the selection of the families in need and the appropriate allotment of activities/trades to them. Although the NIB had full authority in the selection of beneficiaries and allotment of trades, there were certain formalities and processes to be followed at the village level. As per the Policy Guidelines, selection of villages and beneficiaries to be covered under NLUP should preferably be done within the month of July of the preceding year, and the selection can also be done in advance for the next two years to facilitate well preparation on the part of the beneficiaries as well as the line departments. Selection of villages and beneficiaries should normally be followed by campaign and awareness creation taken up in the months of September to November.

Selection of beneficiaries and their trades was to be done carefully based on the condition of the family. The Guidelines stated that a proper format should be prepared, and survey was to be conducted by the government employees and NGOs after giving them proper training on the matter in October of the year preceding the selection of villages and beneficiaries. This survey should cover all the eligible families keeping in view the target and non-target groups as stated in the Policy Manual. The NIB would then consider the survey results submitted from different villages for finalisation of the beneficiaries list and villages to be covered by taking into consideration various factors like topography, temperature, soil condition, market viability, etc.

The Policy Guidelines strives to achieve need based allocation on the number of villages to be covered and the number of beneficiaries in the selected villages. However, the actual implementation experienced that the policy covered all the villages in all the districts simultaneously, while the number of beneficiaries to be assisted was allotted to each village arbitrarily without proper guidelines. In fact, NLUP was the main agenda of the ruling Congress Party in the election and so, the party members in every village became stakeholders with a feeling of ownership. Thus, exclusion of some villages or districts would politically be a risky decision. Consequently, all villages were covered and the number of beneficiaries estimated to be covered in the first phase was distributed to these villages by the NIB according to their population or number of eligible families.

6.7. Delivery of Assistance

Delivery of the assistances was to be made transparently in such a way that the beneficiaries would receive maximum benefit and utilisation. The assistances had to be released as per the notified Calendar of Works on an instalment basis. According to the Policy Guidelines, every beneficiary was required to open a bank account specially meant for the project, and all cash assistances would be deposited in these accounts. However, delivery of cash assistance through bank account depends upon the banking facilities in the concerned villages and areas. As such, if the grant is paid in cash, payment record should be entered clearly in the NLUP Progress Chart, duly signed by the beneficiary, disbursing officer, and the Village Council President (VCP) as witness. In addition, Actual Payee Receipt (APR) would be obtained from every beneficiary receiving the assistance, be it kind or cash. VIKAS PATRIKA had to be issued to each beneficiary and the latter should keep this book ready for check by NLUP Officers and Staff at any time. The purpose of grant, the date, time, and the amount paid should be recorded in this book.

It was a main objective to provide quality seeds for the beneficiaries as part of the material assistance. The concerned department was entrusted with the procurement of seeds and seedlings to be distributed to the beneficiaries, and they would be accountable for any sub-standard seeds and seedlings supplied. There were two major sources of seeds supply, viz., departmentally procured from outside sources and from registered local nurseries. Priority was to be given to the latter for all things being equal.

6.8. Approach to Land Use Planning

6.8.1. *Land Utilisation Targets*

Having clear land use targets should be the beginning of any policy that aims at sustainable land utilisation and cultivation. NLUP is no exception. The importance of having sustainable land use target was recognised at the drafting stage of the programme by taking into consideration the suggestions made by M.S. Swaminathan Research Foundation (1998) for sustainable agricultural and rural development. The actual implementation of the programme saw the requirement of land allotment to the beneficiaries as well as prospective beneficiaries for undertaking land based activities. Although the state revenue laws envisaged land allotment to be made by the State Land Revenue and Settlement Department, the Village Councils (VC) are the practical stakeholders of it. So, the government took necessary steps to prevent unjustified allotment of land in view of the desired land use pattern of the policy. Thus, it was considered necessary that systematic allotment of plots of land be made, which will ensure justice to the landless jhum cultivators in all the villages covered under the scheme. In addition to the distribution of land to the beneficiaries, the project aimed at keeping a large area covered by dense forest so as to create a good environment for the future.

In order to ensure a systematic allotment of land for the implementation of land based activities to each beneficiary, the State NLUP Implementing Board issued a notification in January 2011 for the preparation of Land

Use Plan for all villages. According to the guidelines mentioned in this Notification, every village had to prepare land use plan to ensure the desired pattern of land utilisation as follows:

1. Dense/Rain Forest : 60 per cent.
2. Catchment Area Forest : 10 per cent.
3. Community Supply Reserve : 10 per cent
4. Land based NLUP activities : 15 per cent.
5. Habitation, roads, etc. : 5 per cent

In addition, the DPR of NLUP also contemplated certain initiatives to achieve the above land use pattern. They are — intervention of customary land holding system with sustainable development; conducting detailed survey of land for preparation of land records and settlement; introduction of new landholding, ownership, and management system; and formulation and enactment of new land revenue law. A number of trainings and workshops were organised across the state to ensure the achievement of the desired land use targets. However, it was later realised that most villages did not comply with the guidelines issued by the Government while distributing plots of land for NLUP beneficiaries. Ultimately, the service of the Department of Economics, Mizoram University was engaged to visit all the villages and prepare proper land use plans with the participation of the villagers.

The exercise of participatory land use planning was undertaken by this Department in 456 villages, while villages falling under Autonomous District Councils could not be covered due to the election of local bodies at that time. The supervisors who visited these villages acted as the facilitators of the exercise and tried to ensure the compliance of the notified land use target by the stakeholder villagers. These villagers were given the proposed land use target prepared by themselves in the presence of the village supervisor, and they were made responsible for the achievement of these targets. The existing land use pattern as obtained from the villagers in the exercise is presented in Figure 6.2, while expected pattern upon the successful adoption of the land utilisation plan is also presented in Figure 5.6.

The newly allotted land for NLUP was envisioned to be made out of the current community land, where shifting cultivation had been practised. Reserved forest under different classifications, like village safety reserve,

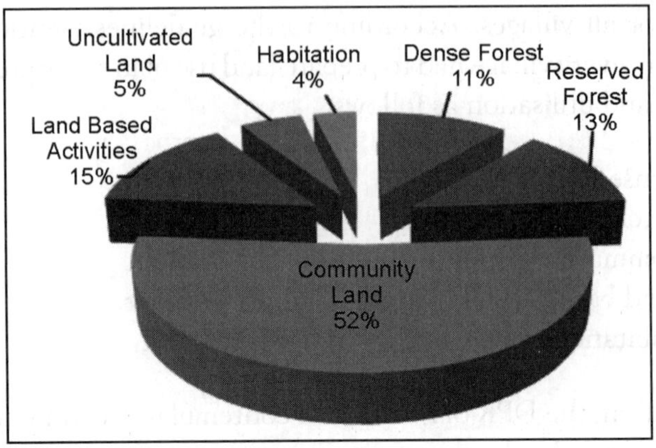

Fig. 6.2: Existing Land Use Pattern (2011)
Source: Rural Land Use Plan, 2011.

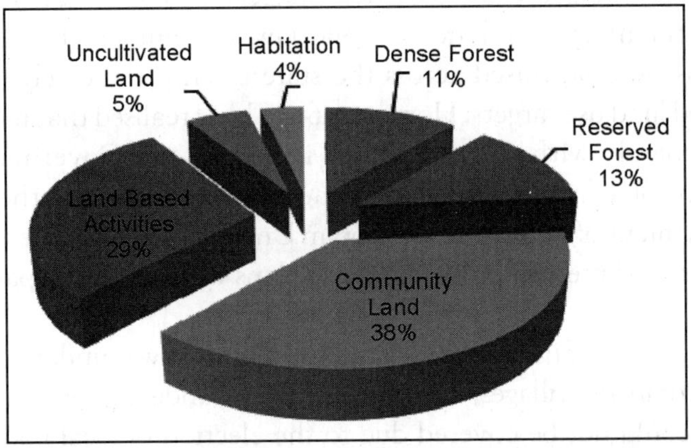

Fig. 6.3: Expected Land Use Pattern
Source: Rural Land Use Plan, 2011

community supply reserve, and protected reserved forests, were all clubbed under *Reserved Forest.* Though there was slight deviation from the official target, success of the participatory land use planning at village levels would result in the emergence of large area under dense/rainfed forest in the coming years. This is subject to the successful implementation of NLUP and sustainable management of forest that comes under the category of *community land*.

6.8.2. *One Crop – One Village*

The NLUP Programme envisaged commercial orientation of agro-horticultural development and targeted its production on a commercial scale. To maximise production of a particular crop, attain economies of scale, and also facilitate marketing, it was planned to introduce a 'One Crop - One Village' concept. Few villages were to be selected for experiment. This programme of 'one crop-one village' was to be done by identifying suitable crops on village-wise cluster basis, and funds were to be earmarked for the development of agro-horticulture sector. The approach was highly desired for the sustainability of land use keeping in view the existence of better scope for further policy intervention towards the success of the scheme. However, the initiative for achieving *'one crop – one village'* approach was unsuccessful, and beneficiaries of the same villages opted for varying activities ranging from agriculture to industries and microenterprises. This resulted in sporadic spread of different beneficiaries in various places undertaking varying degrees of activities and posed a serious hindrance for the formulation of further policy intervention and exit strategy for the scheme.

On realising the multiplicity of trades adopted by beneficiaries from each village and the consequent problems of administration and monitoring work, the NIB in its meeting in the beginning of 2014 decided to revive the approach for the subsequent phases. Kolasib district was the first to embark upon this initiative. As most of the areas falling under the district are suitable for cultivation of Oil Palm, Kolasib was declared an 'Oil Palm District'. In fact, the district is where cultivation of this crop was undertaken at large scale in 2004 under MIP, and the same was continued in NLUP. However, the initiative could not make much headway due to resistance from the beneficiaries who sought the support of a political boss sitting at the decision-making authority. Thus, the concept of 'one crop – one village' could not be realised in a meaningful way.

6.8.3. *Compact Area Approach*

The importance of having common areas where the beneficiaries are clustered for further development in terms of link road construction, market accessibility, etc. was given due attention by the programme. The policy guidelines clearly stated the necessity of having NLUP *Compact Area* in each village where the beneficiaries are clustered. Further, a Notification was made in 2011 that instructed all villages to demarcate the areas to be made as *Compact Area*. All beneficiaries adopting land based activities would be located in one compact area in respect of one village. If that is physically not possible, two or even three compact areas may be identified for the purpose. Ideally, land allotted per beneficiary should not be less than two hectares and should have good source of water for the purpose of irrigation. At the same time, beneficiaries having their own land that is suitable for NLUP activities would not be allotted a separate land.

6.8.4. Cluster Approach

The NIB encouraged cluster approach or crop-zoning in view of the various factors like topography, temperature, soil conditions, etc. for identification of trades/activities. Cluster or Crop Zone would be decided by the Apex Board based on scientific input of subject experts and the Mizoram Remote Sensing Application Centre (MIRSAC). Although the concept was desired for the development of sustainable agriculture in the state, it could not materialise. The actual implementation of the programme saw identification of clusters by Assembly Constituency, rather than by natural factors like topography, soil fertility, slope, etc. Each Assembly Constituency was identified as one cluster irrespective of what trade is suitable in such areas. Number of beneficiaries to be assisted was mostly allocated using the population size without giving much emphasis on the needs and resources of the area. This became one of the major sources of failure which would be analysed in a separate chapter.

6.8.5. Institutionalisation of Land Holding

The beneficiaries were not to be given permanent right of ownership of land unless they utilise the land allotted to them fully for the purpose of which it was allotted. A permanent land pass would be issued by State Revenue Department only on the recommendation of the NIB. The need for having permanent ownership by the poor beneficiaries was imminent for the sustainability of their activities. The failure of the state government to provide sustainable institutional provisions for land protection and ownership led to a rise in land market where land alienation from within the state and tribe emerged in rural areas since the recent past. The poor farmers are the losers in such situations as they have to sell their land to the rich due to family expenditure requirements of medical treatment and education.

The state government had contemplated the issues here and again, and enacted new land laws called The Mizoram Land Revenue Act, 2013. The process of land survey is underway under the funding of Central Plan schemes. However, the linkage of the land survey works and requirement for transfer of land ownership to the beneficiaries as specified in the NLUP Policy Guidelines is highly questionable. It would undoubtedly be a herculean task for the State Revenue Department, having small staff strength, to survey more than one lakh landholdings spread across the state within a short period of time.

6.9. Marketing Policy

It is understood that families engaged in agriculture and allied sector face hardship in marketing their produce. Hence, the task of formulating a successful marketing policy was an essential part of the NLUP Programme. A Marketing Cell, with Chairman, Member Secretary and Members appointed by the government, was constituted under the umbrella of NIB to explore and find the ways and means of marketing the products of the beneficiaries, especially of those under agriculture and allied sectors. The Cell was entrusted with the preparation of a marketing plan for economic emancipation of all the poor families in Mizoram who do not have viable economic opportunities. Reorganisation of fragmented and unorganised existing marketing system for the evolution of sustainable marketing practices was the main objective guiding the formulation of the marketing plan under NLUP.

Some of the areas that were envisioned in the preparation of marketing plan upon the implementation of the programme may be enumerated as follows. First, careful selection of crops is the critical point for the success of a market plan. The beneficiaries would be assisted by experts in their selection of crops. Some of the crops that have relatively better market chain listed out in the policy manual are aloe vera, patchouli, stevia, oil palm, broom grass, passion fruits, grapes, mandarin orange, areca nut, rubber, etc. Although the beneficiaries were given enough freedom in selection of their trades, these crops were generally suggested.

Secondly, creation of marketing infrastructures to facilitate marketing of the produce by the beneficiaries was another area of interest. *One*, wholesale markets would be established at Vairengte, the town neighbouring Assam state, while the same would also be established in all district capitals according to the need and volume of market arrivals. *Two*, attempt was to be made to create a network of market intelligence in Mizoram where vital market information across the country could be accessed via the internet. *Three*, the existing godowns and cold storage facilities at Vairengte, Serchhip, Champhai, and Chhingchhip with capacity of 3500 MT, 500 MT, 1000 MT, and 500 MT respectively would be improved with better operation and maintenance framework and equipment. *Four*, facilities for grading, cleaning, sorting, and packing of the products would be created. *Five*, upgradation and expansion of existing processing units would be taken up. Necessary initiative would be undertaken to enhance the products of bamboo for export venture, and agarbatti industry would also be set up. *Six*, whenever marketing is talked about, the key ingredient for the success of any intervention is the existence of link road for easy transportation of the produce. The programme intended to give priority to filling the major infrastructural gap of market access through construction of link road.

Thirdly, the government would seek ways and means for creation of agriculture and allied produce marketing support system in the form of minimum support price, market intervention scheme, market access initiatives, and transport subsidy. Fourthly, action was proposed to be undertaken for creating Mizoram Trade Brand/Trade Market for certain products exported to other places. Lastly, the policy would attempt to chalk out a system, that is better than the existing one, for sale and processing of bamboos, wood, and forest products so that the people of the state can earn remunerative profit.

6.10. Project Monitoring

There should be an efficient system of monitoring and evaluation for the success of any scheme. The NLUP also, right from its inception, designed comprehensive monitoring framework with the participation of various stakeholders. The main objectives in the design of monitoring framework were (1) Transparency, (2) Social Audit, and (3) Evaluation. Any programme of work and achievement was to be made transparent and accessible to the public, while stakeholders like prominent citizens of the villages, village councils, beneficiaries, etc. would be involved in the process of monitoring. At the same time, information should be made available to the public about the success or failure of the programme. It was expected that the task of evaluation be outsourced to an independent body that can generate unbiased results and observations.

The task of field level monitoring and evaluation was entrusted to the Village Level Monitoring Committee (VLMC). It would monitor the implementation of schemes taken up in the village by conducting field visit in their respective villages, and their observations and recommendations should be submitted to the District Level Monitoring Committee (DLMC), chaired by the Deputy Commissioner (DC). The recommendations of the DLMC are to be submitted to the State Level Monitoring Committee (SLMC). Further, social auditing should be conducted by the VLMC to check the performances and accountabilities of the beneficiaries in their villages.

Another important aspect in the area of monitoring is independent evaluation of the performance of the beneficiaries and the various stakeholders of the scheme. At the start of the project, DJ Consultancy Services Pvt. Limited based in Bhubaneswar, Odisha, was engaged to undertake the task of monitoring and evaluation. However, this firm withdrew quickly due to some technical problems on their part. Upon their withdrawal the second highest bidder in the quotation, NABARD Consultancy Services Ltd. (NABCONS), was awarded the tender. NABCONS had undertaken the monitoring and evaluation of works till the end of the project period. In addition to its regular works of monitoring and evaluation reports submitted to the NIB from time to time, NABCONS also published 'The Mid-Term Assessment of NLUP – Report (MTA)' in 2013. The MTA indicated the direction of the NLUP implementation and provided the extent of success and achievement by various project stakeholders including the beneficiaries. Further, an independent Social Audit was undertaken by the Mizoram Synod Social Front in 2011, which basically evaluated the selection and identification of the beneficiaries.

6.11. Concluding Note

We can say that NLUP 2011 is the biggest project ever adopted in Mizoram for farmers and the poor in terms of its coverage and amount of assistance.

The project envisaged a wide range of activities, land based and other activities, under different participating departments (Line Departments). It also provided comprehensive strategy for funding, project management, monitoring, land use planning, marketing, and infrastructure development. An attractive initiative under NLUP is the convergence of CSS with the project-related activities, especially for infrastructure development. The state government had been implementing developmental schemes under central plan through related government department in a fragmented form since long time back. This resulted in overlapping of schemes of the different departments in many cases without having significant results on its own. For example, Agriculture Department constructs agriculture link road under central plan schemes, while Rural Development Department also constructs link roads under related central schemes like MGNREGA. At the same time, forest link road is also constructed by Forest Department under central scheme for village forest development. If these funding supports received from the centre, which can be used for construction of link roads, are pulled together towards a common target, the schemes would serve meaningful purposes.

Decentralised model of project management system adopted by NLUP is another area of interest. The project management has a four tier system, two at state level (Apex Board and NIB), and one each at district and village levels, while the line departments are the real stakeholders of its implementation. It has the potential to be one of the most successful and attractive democratic project management practices, if implemented efficiently. However, the actual implementation of the project did not show efficient functioning and participation of these stakeholders. Although made functional at the initial stage, the participation of village level committees in further implementation and project monitoring was negligible, mostly due to politicised appointment of members and selection of beneficiaries. Even though it was recognised that their active functioning would be one of the keys to the success of the scheme, they were practically reduced to a mere taker of the decision of the higher authority. This is a serious loophole which could lead to massive failure in the management and monitoring of the project.

The project set out a clear approach to land use planning in view of the need for environment protection, market accessibility of the project area, and to enhance further public intervention schemes. It is unfortunate that approaches such as *one crop – one village*, *cluster approach*, and *compact area approach*, could not be implemented even at the beginning of the project. Implementation of such a massive land use policy without sticking to proper set of strategies in its allocation and management at the village level is a risky initiative, which could result in cultivation of diverse crops in isolated locations. This can complicate the challenge of making further public intervention schemes on crop maintenance, marketing, and sustainable land resource management practices in the future. Instead of moving the people out of it, it can dislocate the well-organised practice of the shifting cultivation, making it more harmful than it traditionally was.

7

PROGRESS AND ACHIEVEMENT OF NLUP 2011

7.1. Introduction

The 'Comprehensive project under New Land Use Policy for sustained economic development and the uplift of the poor in Mizoram', in short *NLUP 2011*, encompassed a wide range of activities and funding patterns. It is an improvement over the previous projects that strive for sustainable land utilisation and put an end to the practice of shifting cultivation, in terms of coverage, funding, and project management. It was the adopted Flagship Programme of the Congress Party in power after the General Election in 2008. Although the ground work for its implementation started in the beginning of 2009, it could not be taken up quickly mostly due to the time taken for approval and release of fund by Planning Commission. The Detailed Project Report (DPR) was submitted to the Planning Commission in June 2009, and finally the Cabinet Committee on Economic Affairs (CCEA) chaired by the Prime Minister, approved the DPR on the 2nd of July 2010. This was followed by the release of the first instalment. It was finally launched on 11 January 2011, and the day is declared *Kuthnathawktute Ni* (Farmers' Day) to be officially celebrated every year. The programme was scheduled for a period of five years starting from 2010-11 to 2014-15. The Apex Board on its sitting dated 19 May 2014 decided on the continuation of the programme for another five years after 2014-15.

The project is implemented by a host of eight participating Government Departments, called *Line Departments*. In addition to these, Urban

Development and Poverty Alleviation (UD & PA) also became a designated Line Department for some industrial trades in Aizawl city area since 2012-13. As stated in the previous chapter, there are a number of stakeholders or committees for the project management at village level, district level, and state level. At the state level, the NLUP Implementing Board (NIB) is the executing agency and at the highest level is the Apex Committee chaired by the Chief Minister for policy decision regarding fund allocation, approval of action plan and link to the Central Government. The project is broadly divided into three major components — development, management, and infrastructure, and a separate fund allocation was made to each of these components. A distinct feature of this project is the Convergence Scheme where the NLUP activities would be converged with the initiatives of CSS, mostly in the provision of necessary infrastructure for the sustenance of the scheme and marketing of the products.

7.2. Component Wise Fund Allocation

As stated, the financial allocation for different activities under NLUP as approved by CCEA is broadly divided into three major heads — development, infrastructure, and management. All the material and cash assistance given directly or indirectly to the beneficiaries comes under the 'development component'. The project envisioned creation of necessary infrastructures to facilitate the success and marketing of the scheme. Such expenditures are under 'infrastructure component,' and they are mostly to be made from convergence scheme of Centrally Sponsored Schemes (CSS). At the same time, efficient management and monitoring of the scheme is necessary. All the expenditures related to the administration and monitoring of the project are clubbed together under 'management component'. The breakup of the annual fund allocation to each of these components is presented in Table 7.1.

Table 7.1 shows that the main chunk of the project fund goes to development component, basically assistance to the beneficiaries. It constituted more than around 90 per cent of the total fund allocation. Management expenditure constituted less than five per cent of the project cost (i.e. 3.97 per cent on average). Fund earmarked for development of necessary infrastructure constituted less than 10 per cent of the total fund, even as low as 2.14 per cent in 2011-12. The approach adopted in implementing NLUP may be gauged from the distribution of the project

Table 7.1
Component-Wise Financial Allocation under NLUP in Mizoram

Year	*Management*	*Infrastructure*	*Development*	*Total*
Amount (Rs. Crores)				
2010-11	15.62	20.49	198.71	234.82
2011-12	10.00	5.00	219.00	234.00
2012-13	10.00	25.00	335.00	370.00
2013-14	12.00	18.00	340.00	370.00
2014-15	15.00	33.00	322.00	370.00
Total	62.62	101.49	1414.71	1578.82
Percentage Share				
2010-11	6.65	8.73	84.62	100.00
2011-12	4.27	2.14	93.59	100.00
2012-13	2.70	6.76	90.54	100.00
2013-14	3.24	4.86	91.89	100.00
2014-15	4.05	8.92	87.03	100.00
Total	3.97	6.43	89.61	100.00

Source: NIB, *Agenda Notes for 13th Apex Board Meeting*, Dated 29th May 2014.

fund among the three components. Direct assistance was given a lion's share, while initiative for infrastructure development was minimal. The project intended to uplift the poor beneficiaries by giving them the required cash and material assistance to enhance their production thereby ensuring better earning, rather than by providing basic infrastructure to sustainably improve their cultivation practice and its marketing.

7.3. Financial Achievement

Sector-wise fund allocation was made every financial year from 2010-11 to finance the developmental activities under NLUP. The criteria for fund allocation to each sector were the physical achievements in the previous years and the existing trend of trade selection by the newly selected beneficiaries. Fund allocated to a particular department can also spill over to the next financial year because assistance has to be made on an instalment basis for most of the activities/trades. Thus, financial achievements are cumulative achievements, rather than that of a particular financial year. Though no separate allocation was made for the financial year of 2015-16 as the project had completed five years, actual expenditure was spill over of the previous years'. Likewise, it is expected that the flow of assistance would continue until all the instalments are received by the selected beneficiaries. Annual fund allocation and achievement for all NLUP line departments is presented in Table 7.2, while Figure 7.1 summarises the cumulative achievement of these departments till 2016.

The cumulative financial achievement of all the sectors presented in Figure 7.1 shows that the overall achievement rate is only 61.11 per cent. It is surprising to observe that almost 40 per cent of the approved amount for the project could not be spent within a span of five years. Late release of fund from Planning Commission may in fact be the main reason behind this slow progress. However, the situation is more indicative of an inefficient management system to deliver the assistance to the beneficiaries within the stipulated time frame. Surprisingly, the key sector of the project, i.e. agriculture, is the second lowest in terms of financial achievement. At the same time, the achievement rate of fisheries (87.29 per cent) is the highest. The project had an in-built system necessitating the assistance to be delivered on an instalment basis as per a notified Calendar of Works. So, the number of instalments required for completion of the assistance may be another reason for the slow progress of financial achievement.

It is observed from Table 7.2 that expenditure under NLUP project in the first year was only Rs. 36.83 crore, which increased to Rs. 217.18 crore in the second year, and up to May 2016, a total of Rs. 857 crore was to be spent. This may be taken as a big achievement of the state government in implementing its flagship NLUP scheme, though the actual expenditure is well below the approved amount. The trends of financial allocation and achievement as presented in Table 7.2 reveals the declining importance of agriculture sector with increasing importance of animal husbandry and industrial sectors. The same trend is also reflected in the financial achievement in the lower panel of the table. Annual allocation for agriculture sector decreased from Rs. 75 crore in 2010-11 to Rs. 47.75 crore in 2014-15, while the allocation for AH & Vety increased significantly from Rs. 28.32 crore to Rs. 110.97 crore during the same period. In fact, the NLUP project envisioned promotion of agriculture sector for self-sufficiency in food production. However, the trend of financial achievement does not indicate the move in that direction, where the key sector towards it was given lesser importance year after year.

Table 7.2
Sector-Wise Annual Financial Allocation and Achievement of NLUP

Rs. In Crore

Sector/Department	*2010-11*	*2011-12*	*2012-13*	*2013-14*	*2014-15*	*2015-16*	*Total*
Allocation							
Agriculture	75.52	–	62.56	60.3	47.75	–	246.13
Horticulture	52.23	17.34	82.84	78.18	28.4	–	258.99
Soil & Water Conservation	14.16	26.86	33.05	31.5	24.27	–	129.84
Sericulture	5	1.2	8.56	4.05	2.5	–	21.31
Fisheries	3.84	10.6	8.9	5	9.1	–	37.44
Environment & Forest	10.12	1.62	15.33	6.35	5.53	–	38.95
Animal Husbandry & Veterinary	28.32	73.25	63	85.4	110.97	–	360.94
Industries	11	90.19	58.55	55.82	61.33	–	276.89
UD&PA	–	–	4.6	14.9	13.34	–	32.84
Total	**200.19**	**221.06**	**337.39**	**341.5**	**303.19**	**–**	**1403.33**
Achievement							
Agriculture	11.79	47.06	30.84	35.6	11.56	44.66	136.85
Horticulture	12.47	43.4	32.68	48.45	29.56	34.31	166.56
Soil & Water Conservation	–	19.98	20.36	26.61	12.16	7.58	86.69
Sericulture	5	1.2	8.56	2.09	–	–	16.85
Fisheries	–	–	14.47	14.95	3.26	–	32.68
Environment & Forest	4.32	6.86	10.55	5.91	1.29	3.66	32.59
Animal Husbandry & Veterinary	–	46.35	56.65	63.83	28.64	–	195.47
Industries	3.25	52.33	43.39	39.21	19.58	9.21	166.97
UD&PA	–	–	4.33	11.94	3.16	3.49	22.92
Total	**36.83**	**217.18**	**221.83**	**248.59**	**109.21**	**102.91**	**857.58**

Source: NLUP Implementing Board, Government of Mizoram, Dated 6.5.2016.

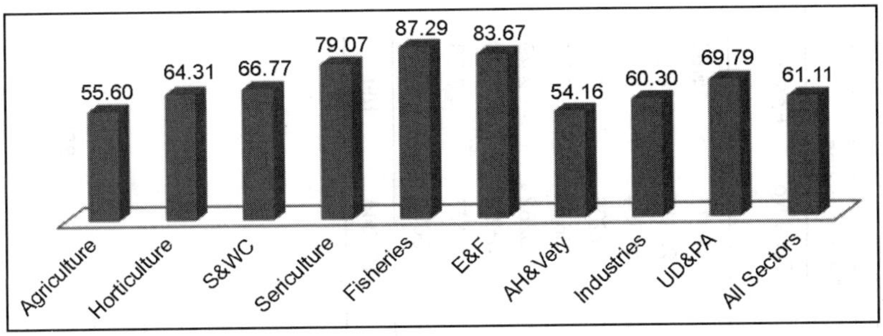

Fig. 7.1: Financial Achievement Percentage up to May 2016 (%)

7.4. Physical Achievement

Selection of the beneficiaries for NLUP was done in a phased manner, and assistance was delivered to the selected beneficiaries on an instalment basis according to the periodic requirement for the completion of the trade they adopted. It was expected to launch the programme in the beginning of the financial year 2010-11. However, it was officially kicked off only towards the later part of this financial year on 14 January 2011 due to the time taken by the Planning Commission for approval of the project and release of fund. Thus, those who were selected during 2010-11 were able to start the actual work only after they received the assistance in the beginning of the financial year 2011-12. Selection and finalisation of the new beneficiaries for the Second Phase was initiated towards the end of 2011-12 and the beginning of 2012-13. Practically the second phase beneficiaries were selected during the financial year 2012-13. The Urban Development and Poverty Alleviation (UD & PA) also entered into the scheme as a line department to cover industrial activities in Aizawl city with the start of the second phase. Thus, the process of beneficiary selection could be completed in four phases in a span of five years starting from 2010-11 to 2014-15. The phase-wise distribution of NLUP beneficiaries is presented in Table 7.3.

A total of 1,32,044 families could be covered by NLUP during the five years of its implementation. This is much higher than the targeted number of beneficiaries as given in the original DPR of the project basically due to the permission granted by the Planning Commission to cover an additional number of 35000 families beyond the original target of 1.2 lakh families. As the State Government decided to continue the programme till 2018 by making financial allocation from the state budget, some new beneficiaries

Table 7.3
Physical Achievement of NLUP among the different Line Departments (Sectors)

		No. of Beneficiaries					
Sl. No	Department	1st Phase (2010-11)	2nd Phase (2012-13)	3rd Phase (2013-14)	4th Phase (2014-15)	Total No	Percent
1.	Agriculture	6052	7576	4383	1900	19911	15.08
2.	Horticulture	9327	8592	4049	1845	23813	18.03
3.	Soil & Water Conservation	5389	3545	2022	898	11854	8.98
4.	Sericulture	826	1058	233	89	2206	1.67
5.	Fisheries	1447	1131	717	359	3654	2.77
6.	Environment & Forest	1409	1191	474	208	3282	2.49
7.	Animal Husbandry & Veterinary	9923	12886	9536	4709	37054	28.06
8.	Industries	10730	7632	5936	2879	27177	20.58
9.	UD&PA	–	1416	1244	433	3093	2.34
	Total	**45103**	**45027**	**28594**	**13320**	**132044**	**100**

Source: NLUP Implementing Board, Govt. of Mizoram, dated 29.05.2014.

are expected to be covered even after the completion of the project period in 2014-15. However, substantial addition to the number of beneficiaries is unlikely as the funding support from the Centre would have ended.

The largest contributor of the overall physical achievement of NLUP is the AH & Vety sector contributing 28.06 per cent followed by industrial sector under Industries Department and UD & PA which amounts to 22.92 per cent, while the contribution of Sericulture is the lowest at 1.67 per cent. The major sectors as per the physical achievement are AH & Vety, industries, agriculture, horticulture, and soil and water conservation; while sericulture, fisheries, environment and forest are the less significant sectors. Against the target of 5.42 per cent of the total number of beneficiaries, the industrial sector contributed around 23 per cent of the beneficiaries. Similarly, the physical achievement of animal husbandry sector at 28.06 per cent is significantly higher than the targeted percentage of 15.72 per cent. The relatively higher achievement of the two sectors is at the expense of the agriculture and horticultural sector. The physical target of the agriculture and horticulture was 50.33 per cent, while the achievement rate was only 33.11 per cent.

Detailed physical achievements under land based and industrial sectors are presented in Table 7.4 and Table 7.5 respectively. The former represent those beneficiaries who require land for undertaking their trades, while the latter are meant for manufacturing and services that do not require much land for their trades. More than 84 per cent of the beneficiaries under agriculture sector adopted wet rice cultivation (WRC), that is, 44 per cent and 40 per cent for WRC-I and WRC-II respectively. Thus, WRC alone constituted 16.45 per cent and 12.68 per cent of the beneficiaries under agriculture sector and the total number of beneficiaries respectively. The project divided Wet Rice Cultivation (WRC) into two, according to the slope of the land where it is to be developed. Land having a slope below 10 per cent and 10-25 per cent are categorised as WRC-I and WRC-II respectively. The latter can simply be called Hill Terracing. WRC-I constituted more than 6.64 per cent of the total number of beneficiaries, while 6.04 per cent is constituted by WRC-II. It may be noted that one of the main objectives of NLUP is to put an end to wasteful shifting cultivation; and to develop all suitable land for WRC to attain self-sufficiency in rice and vegetables (NLUP Manual, 2009). In fact, the desired objective is reflected by the physical achievement ratio to some extent. However, the

Table 7.4
Trade-Wise Physical Achievement of NLUP under Agriculture & Allied Sectors and Other Land based Sectors

No. of Beneficiaries

Department	*Trades*	*2010-11*	*2012-13*	*2013-14*	*2014-15*	*Total*
Agriculture	WRC-I	3345	2914	1704	804	8767
	WRC-II	1950	3073	2090	863	7976
	Oil Palm	403	1260	451	176	2290
	Sugarcane	354	329	138	57	878
Horticulture	Grape	324	231	45	19	619
	Passion fruit	166	133	78	40	417
	M. Orange	4396	4142	2007	922	11467
	Aloevera	23	6	7	3	39
	Arecanut	2753	2515	1087	567	6922
	Pineapple	1217	1023	585	181	3006
	Chayote	285	131	30	18	464
	Tung	141	206	109	20	476
	Tea	22	205	84	73	384
	Mango			17	2	19
Sericulture	Mulberry	826	1058	233	89	2206
Soil & WC	Broom	3858	2697	1516	691	8762
	Rubber	659	436	265	114	1474
	Coffee	872	412	241	93	1618
Fisheries	Aquaculture	1447	1131	717	359	3654
AH &Vety	Dairy	949	380	254	134	1717
	Piggery	5330	7006	5453	2753	20542
	Mithun	1856	1141	603	327	3927
	Poultry	1788	4359	3226	1495	10868
E&F	Bamboo	1409	1191	474	208	3282
Total		**34373**	**35979**	**21414**	**10008**	**101774**

Source: NLUP Implementing Board, Government of Mizoram, dated 29.5.2014.

percentage is quite low to bring about commendable achievement of these objectives. This may be interpreted as a significant deviation of the physical achievement from the desired targets.

Horticultural development is the main strategy for bringing an end to the shifting cultivation under NLUP after wet rice cultivation. The policy envisaged that 24 per cent of the beneficiaries would take up horticultural trades, while the achievement showed that only 18.03 per cent did so.

Table 7.5
Trade-Wise Physical Achievements of NLUP under Industries and Service Sector

Department	*Trades*	*No. of Beneficiaries*				
		2010-11	*2012-13*	*2013-14*	*2014-15*	*Total*
Industries	Autorickshaw	69	194	216	87	566
	Automobile Works	284	113	73	22	492
	Bakery	89	61	33	16	199
	Beauty Parlour	145	11	25	16	197
	Black-Smithy	165	116	61	21	363
	Broom Making-I	77	72	16	4	169
	Cane & Bamboo Works	29	12	1	2	44
	Carpentry-I	1488	815	550	294	3147
	Carpentry-II	219	232	110	42	603
	Chow Making	93	24	19	6	142
	Desktop Publishing	152	83	152	85	472
	Electronic Repair	238	80	35	20	373
	Hair Cutting	128	49	38	17	232
	Handloom	181	102	159	95	537
	Knitting	32	3	1	1	37
	Leather & Hood Works	18	9	0	1	28
	Petty Trade-I	4321	3573	3135	1594	12623
	Petty Trade-IV	78	50	37	14	179
	Photography	135	60	81	44	320
	Rice Hulling	224	101	39	36	400
	Square Agarbati-I	54	17	2	1	74
	Steel Fabrication	121	70	49	21	261
	Tailoring	1110	307	389	162	1968
	Special Micro Enterprise (SME)	1161	1447	687	265	3560
UD&PA	Automobile Works	–	89	51	20	160
	Beauty Parlour	–	91	65	19	175
	Desktop Publishing	–	161	279	90	530
	Electronic Repair	–	107	100	32	239
	Hair Cutting	–	46	18	4	68
	Knitting	–	8	6	2	16
	Leather & Hood Works	–	8	12	3	23
	Photography & Videography	–	63	129	43	235
	Shoe Repairing	–	29	8	6	43
	Tailoring	–	814	576	214	1604
Total		**10611**	**9017**	**7152**	**3299**	**30079**

Source: NLUP Implementing Board, Government of Mizoram, dated 29.05.2014.

Major horticultural trades according to their contribution in the total number of beneficiaries in the sector are mandarin orange (48.15 per cent), areca nut (29.07 per cent), and pineapple (12.62 per cent), while their contribution to the total beneficiaries in the entire sectors are 8.68 per cent, 5.24 per cent, and 2.28 per cent respectively. These crops had been cultivated in the state for a very long time, and the climatic condition is also suitable for their successful cultivation. Addition of this much of new families in the cultivation to the existing capacity has the potential to boost the entire horticulture production in the near future.

Broom stick cultivation under Soil & Water Conservation Department is another major land based trade which has 8762 families under it (i.e. 6.64 per cent of the total beneficiaries). Higher than expected number of beneficiaries selected piggery trade. 20542 adopted the trade, that is, more than 15 per cent of the beneficiaries across the different sectors adopted piggery. Poultry, which has 10868 beneficiaries, constituted 8.23 per cent of all the beneficiaries across the nine sectors. Thus, the two trades of piggery and poultry under Animal Husbandry and Veterinary (AH & Vety) constituted more than 25 per cent of the total beneficiaries. This is significantly higher than the physical target for AH & Vety sector at 15.72 per cent. The physical achievement observed here are extremely high taking into consideration the physical target of the programme, which would also pose serious challenge in monitoring of the programme. The main reason for the higher proportion of the beneficiaries adopting piggery and poultry trade is because the poor beneficiaries in urban and semi-urban areas are forced to choose these trades as they do not have the required land for undertaking land based activities.

Table 7.5 presents the physical achievement of NLUP for industrial trades under Industries Department and UD&PA (for Aizawl City area). There are 24 major trades in which there is one major trade named SME encompassing vast areas of industrial and service activities that cannot be easily put into single trade. However, the amount of assistance under SME is relatively less. The most significant trade under industrial sector is Petty Trade-I with 12623 beneficiaries which accounted for 42.97 per cent and 9.56 per cent of the beneficiaries under industries and all sectors respectively. Petty Trade is divided into four categories: Grocery shop with a total assistance amount of Rs. 1.2 lakh is categorised as Petty Trade-I, Vegetable Shop having assistance amount of Rs. 60,000 as Petty Trade-II; Tea Stall

(Rs. 60,000) as Petty Trade-III; and Way-side-food stall with Rs. 1.2 lakh assistance as Petty Trade-IV. Interestingly, there were no beneficiaries who adopted Petty Trade-II & III most probably due to lower amount of assistance.

A common problem faced by urban beneficiaries is unavailability of working space. Mostly, the urban poor who need assistance are living in small rented houses without land of their own. This restricts them from pursuing activities of their interest. Selection of beneficiary was done simply by making arbitrary (or proportional) allotment to the administrative cluster (MLA Constituency) without taking into consideration the socio-economic status of the people in that area. Thus, there could not be a clear cut yardstick for the selection of beneficiaries, although it was desired to be done on need basis. Since the viability of the proposed trade and availability of work space, skill base, etc., were not given enough weightage in the selection of beneficiaries, the poor beneficiaries could not make much headway in their trades. Large number of the urban beneficiaries tended to choose trades that do not require much skill and space, or trades that could be started even within the residential house, but carried higher amount of cash assistance. Consequently, there are large number of beneficiaries who adopted petty trade. Since there cannot be a yardstick for monitoring and measurement of the success or failure, it seemed like making money in an easy way. This situation has the potential to pull down the success rate of the entire programme to a great extent.

Another major trade under Industries Department is tailoring which have 3572 beneficiaries. That is, 11.88 per cent and 2.71 per cent of industrial and total NLUP beneficiaries respectively. The number is quite reasonable taking into account the requirement to meet the local demand, and the evenly spread of market demand across the villages of the state. However, this trade requires skill on the part of the beneficiaries. Another trade requiring skill is Carpentry-I which has 3147 beneficiaries, and is also a major trade under industrial sector. Such network of families doing carpentry work in an unorganised form has to depend on local demand, rather than the open competition in the outside world. However, if this much of beneficiaries are evenly distributed in the villages and towns, the number may be sufficient enough to cater the need of local demand.

There are 3560 beneficiaries assisted under Special Micro Enterprise (SME) scheme of Industries Department. SME occupied the third position of industrial trades in terms of number of beneficiaries. There are 40 trades under SME, which are basically small businesses and manufacturing of food items, artistic items, automobile related activities, etc. The maximum amount of assistance for these trades is Rs. 50,000. The SME schemes up to March 2016 are listed in Table 7.6.

Table 7.6
Schemes under Special Micro Enterprises (SME) trade of NLUP

S. No.	*Name of Trades (Schemes)*	*S. No.*	*Name of Trades (Schemes)*
1.	Book binding	2.	Butchery & Fish selling (Sa sat)
3.	Candle making	4.	Collection & Selling of sand and stone chips
5.	Crushing of sugarcane	6.	Dry cleaning (home scale)
7.	Extraction of fruit juice	8.	Fermentation of Pork (Sa-um)
9.	Fermentation of Soyabean (Bekang um)	10.	Fire-arm repairing
11.	Handicrafts	12.	Making of aluminium pot
13.	Making of artificial flowers	14.	Making of Mizo Drum
15.	Mini-Stone quarrying	16.	On Call Painting
17.	On call-automech works	18.	On call-carpentry
19.	On call-electro-mechanic work	20.	On call-mechanic/plumbering
21.	Operation of vehicle garage	22.	Pickle making
23.	Preparation & Sale of Mizo Chhangban	24.	Processing & Selling of Betelnut
25.	Processing & Selling of Ice-cream	26.	Processing of limestone
27.	Puncture Works	28.	Road Side Hawker
29.	Selling of Mizo Puan	30.	Servicing of Automobiles
31.	Smoke Meat Making (Sa-rep)	32.	Trade related micro enterprise
33.	Turmeric Grinding	34.	Watch Repairing
35.	Petty Trade II (vegetable shop)	36.	Broom making I
37.	Petty Trade III (Tea Stall)	38.	Square Agarbati Stick Making III
39.	Broom Making II	40.	Shoe Repairing (Home base)

Source: Directorate of Industries, Government of Mizoram, *Achievement of NLUP Under Industries Sector, 2016.*

The assistance made through SME schemes are meant basically for enhancement of the beneficiaries in their existing occupations without imposing any specific trade for them. So, the number of activities can be increased based on the need of the beneficiaries subject to the maximum limit of Rs. 50,000. The SME trade is thus basically a livelihood promotion programme rather than an attempt to shift the beneficiaries out of their existing occupation for new activities. There was no notified Calendar of

Work for the delivery of the assistance for all schemes falling under SME, and the nodal department (Industries) is entrusted to make decision on how the assistance is to be delivered, including whether in one go or on an instalment basis.

7.5. NLUP Convergence Scheme

A distinctive strategy adopted in the implementation of NLUP is the *Convergence Scheme.* The Convergence Scheme is an initiative to emerge coordinated effort among the various government departments that implement various Centrally Sponsored Scheme (CSS) towards a common development goal. The initiative is to converge NLUP with the ongoing CSS so as to avoid duplication of works. In fact, different government departments were implementing CSS suitable to them on their own without giving much consideration on what the other departments are doing. For example, link roads are constructed by Rural Development (RD) Department under MGNREGA scheme; Environment and Forest also construct link road under fund for village forest development committee; and so on. Such situations often result in duplication of works which are meant for more or less the same purpose. The successful convergence of these schemes would pull the resources together in a meaningful way towards the desired objectives, not only for creation of assets but also for its further maintenance. The CSS converged with NLUP are Integrated Scheme of Oilseeds, Pulses, Oil Palm, and Maize (ISOPOM), Technology Mission (TM), National Mission on Medicinal Plants (NMMP), National Bamboo Mission (NBM), Mahatma Gandhi National Rural Employment Guarantee Act (MGNREGA), National Fisheries Development Board (NFDB), and Ministry of New and Renewable Energy (MNRE).

The flow of fund from CSS for development and infrastructure components of NLUP during the first four years of implementation are presented in Table 7.7 and Table 7.8 respectively. A total of Rs. 110.34 crore was allocated from CSS fund for the developmental expenditure of NLUP for a period of five years. Out of this, only Rs. 39.92 crore could be expended, and thus the achievement rate is 36.18 per cent only. The expenditure made from CSS for development component was normally meant for seeds and material supply, cash assistance for jungle clearance, weeding and other farm maintenance in addition to the fund received from

Additional Central Assistance (ACA). The allocation of CSS convergence scheme for development component is highest in case of Technology Mission with a total allocation of Rs. 52.99 crore, and out of this, Rs. 29.08 crore was achieved. Thus, the achievement rate is 54.88 per cent. Among the five CSS that are converged with the programme, financial achievement is highest in case of Technology Mission (54.88 per cent), while it is lowest in Rubber Board and Coffee Board (6.25 per cent).

Table 7.7
Fund Flow from CSS for Development Component under NLUP Convergence Scheme

Rs. in Crore

Sl. No	CSS under convergence	Total Targets for 5 Years	Achievement upto 31.3.2015	Achievement Percent
1.	ISOPOM (Agriculture)	12.90	3.40	26.36
2.	Technology Mission (Horticulture)	52.99	29.08	54.88
3.	NFDB (Fisheries)	15.00	1.68	11.20
4.	Rubber & Coffee Boards (S&WC)	12.00	0.75	6.25
5.	National Bamboo Mission (Forest)	17.45	5.01	28.71
	Total	**110.34**	**39.92**	**36.18**

Source: NLUP Implementing Board, Government of Mizoram, Dated 18.8.2016.

Table 7.8
Status of Fund Flow from CSS for Infrastructure Development under NLUP Convergence Scheme

Rs. in Crore

Sl. No.	Works under CSS convergence	Total Target for 5 Years	Achievement upto 31.3.2015	Achievement Percent
1.	Agriculture Link Road (MGNREGA)	772.6	348.26	45.08
2.	Water Harvesting (MGNREGA)	87.05	107.47	123.46
3.	BNRGSK (MREGA)	–	72.74	–
4..	Rural Godown (BBRGF & IWMP)	27.9	2.43	8.71
5.	Hydroger	2.63	-	0.00
6.	Water Harvesting (Entry Point) under IWMP	–	12.47	–
7.	Ice Plant	0.32	0.00	0.00
	Total	**890.5**	**543.37**	**61.02**

Source: NLUP Implementing Board, Government of Mizoram, Dated 18.8.2016.

Creation of the necessary infrastructure should be the key to sustain the success of the scheme. Table 7.8 presents the fund flow from CSS for infrastructure development under the convergence scheme of NLUP. It can be observed that Rs. 890.5 crore was allocated for five years, out of which Rs. 543.37crore could be utilised, thus showing an achievement rate of 61.67 per cent for infrastructure development. Among the funding source for infrastructure development, the contribution of MGNREGA was highest at Rs. 859.65 crore which is 96.54 per cent of the total allocation; while it constituted 97.26 per cent of the total achievement. Agriculture Link Road remains the main effort of infrastructure creation under NLUP convergence scheme. An amount of Rs. 772.6 crore was allocated, and Rs. 348.26 crore could be achieved out of this allocation. The dominance of link road among the activities taken up for infrastructure development is justifiable considering the hilly topography of the state where most of the agricultural lands are not easily accessible from the existing network of roads. The successful construction and maintenance of these link roads would help improve the market access of the agricultural produce of the farmers.

Lack of water harvesting technology and infrastructure remains to be the problems faced by farmers in Mizoram. The state has heavy rainfall during monsoon, while the span of dry season lasts for almost eight months, starting from October till May of the next year. Most of the springs that have water flow during rainy season dry up during the dry season. So, farm maintenance during the dry season becomes a challenge due to insufficient water sources. The significance of watershed development and water harvesting may be understood from these natural events. The financial achievement for water harvesting was much higher than the amount allocated for a period of five years. It was Rs. 107.47 crore against the total allocation of Rs. 87.05 crore (i.e.123.46 per cent of the allocation). In addition, rural storehouse or godowns to be used by beneficiaries were also constructed through BNRGSK scheme under the convergence scheme, though its allocation was not made initially. Similarly, the fund for water harvesting under IWMP was also converged with the scheme without prior allocation. However, there was zero achievement for installation of hydroger and ice plant that had a total target of Rs. 2.63 crore and Rs. 32 lakh respectively.

One observation related to infrastructure development is the difference in the perception of the general public between the NLUP initiatives on developmental expenditure that are used for beneficiary assistances and the creation of necessary infrastructures through convergence scheme. Deliveries of the direct assistances, cash or kind, given to the beneficiaries were normally made known to the general public and were publicised through print and visual media. The beneficiaries were also made aware of the amount of the assistance they are supposed to receive, while the officials were made accountable in the delivery of the beneficiary assistance. However, information about the creation of the assets, selection of location, etc. to be undertaken from the Convergence Scheme was not made available to the public. So, a sense of ownership is hard to come by from the beneficiaries of NLUP as well as the stakeholder (line departments). Further, there is no mechanism mentioned in the policy guidelines for monitoring and evaluation of infrastructure development. The task was simply left to the department concerned with the funding sources. It is necessary that such a big initiative with an expenditure of more than Rs. 543.37crore be made accountable to the NLUP policy framework.

7.6. Input Supply Chain under NLUP

Input supply under NLUP may be broadly divided into two — cash assistance and material assistance (or, financial assistance and assistance in kind). Cash assistance was normally delivered directly to the beneficiaries by the concerned line department as per the Calendar of Works through bank transfer wherever there are banking facilities. This was meant for meeting the expenditure required for periodic activities in undertaking their selected trades to which the beneficiaries were given freedom either to hire labour or do the work themselves. They were also given the freedom to procure materials required for accomplishment of these periodic activities. Cash assistance was not to be taken as mere cash assistance, but each amount was made for specific purpose or activity. The activities and amount of cash assistance to each activity for WRC-I under agriculture may be cited here to make the purpose of cash assistance clearer:

1. Jungle clearance, and contour survey — Rs. 15200
2. Land levelling — Rs. 44,800
3. Construction of field channels, drainages, etc. — Rs. 24,000
4. Agriculture inputs (seeds, fertilizers, etc.) — Rs. 20,000
5. Agri. inputs and operational cost for rabi crops — Rs. 16,000
6. Total — Rs. 1,20,000

At the same time, material assistances are those that are required by the beneficiaries, but cannot be easily accessed by them as they are not sold at the farmers' doorstep. The material includes seeds, fingerlings, GI Wires, machinery, etc. Though the beneficiaries may be able to get such materials at the local markets, their quality cannot be assured. So, the government intended to fill such access gap. The various authorities governing the input supply under NLUP is presented in a chart form in Figure 7.2.

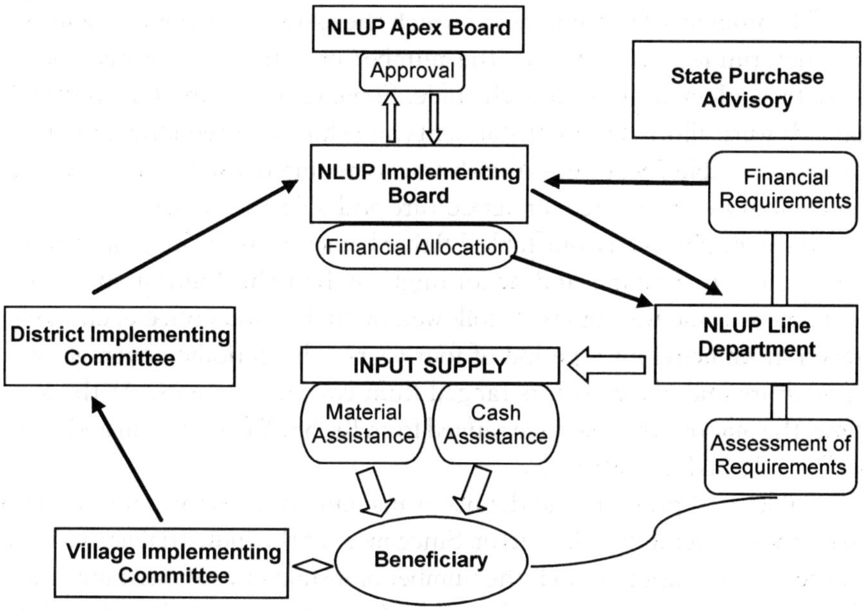

Fig. 7.2: Flow of Input Supply Chain under NLUP in Mizoram

The input supply chain management system of NLUP may be summarised as follows. Firstly, the process of beneficiary selection is the starting point. The task of identifying families to be assisted under NLUP is entrusted to the Village Level Implementing Committee. This committee submits its report to the district implementing committee, for onward submission to the NIB for approval. Secondly, after finalisation of trades for all selected beneficiaries, the NIB instructs the concerned line department for assessment of the required quantity of material and cash assistances to each beneficiary. This is submitted to the NIB for financial allocation and further submission to Apex Board for approval. Thirdly, the

NIB gives nod to the line department to call for quotation for supply of material inputs like machineries, equipments, etc. after all the proposal for amount of assistance is approved by the Apex Board. Fourthly, the selection of suppliers for these material inputs was to be done by the State Purchase Advisory Board (SPAB) chaired by the Chief Secretary. The SPB would then submit its recommendation to the NIB for approval and necessary action. Finally, it is the line department that delivers all the input supply to the beneficiaries.

The number of instalments to which the assistance would be delivered was determined according to the number of activities required for the smooth implementation of each trade. Some crops having long gestation periods were allotted more instalments and thus, covered longer period of assistance. Table 7.9 presents the abstract of required instalments, coverage, and amount of assistance for agriculture and allied activities.

It can be observed from Table 7.9 that bamboo has the longest gestation period, i.e. five years, and accordingly, it had the highest number of instalment (nine instalments), followed by rubber and coffee each having seven instalments for a period of four years. The periodic coverage of all agriculture and allied sectors ranged from two to five years. At the same time, the amount of assistance ranged from Rs. 88,000 for broom and coffee to Rs. 1.36 lakh for WRC-II.

Table 7.10 presents the details of instalment, amount, and period of assistance under industries sector. Since most of the industrial activities do not require gestation period, the number of instalments of assistance range from one to three with a periodic range of one to two years. Beneficiaries of auto rickshaw, DTP, and photography were given their assistance in one go, while cane and bamboo, carpentry, petty trades, shoe repairing, and square agarbatti stick making were given in two instalments. All the remaining trades were given in three instalments within a period of two years.

To examine the periodic flow of assistance to the beneficiaries, the case of First Phase beneficiaries under Horticulture Department may be examined. The result is presented in Table 7.11. Cumulative achievement of the department in giving assistance to the beneficiaries presented in this table is summarised in Figure 7.3 and Figure 7.4 for trades with five instalments and four instalments respectively. Generally, beneficiaries were given the first two instalments in the first year, which constitute 30 per

Table 7.9
Abstract of the Released Assistance for Various Activities under Agriculture and Allied Sector

Sector	*Trade*	*No. of Instalment*	*Coverage (Yrs.)*	*Amount (Rs. in lakh)*
Agriculture	WRC-I	5	2	1.20
	WRC-II	5	2	1.36
	Oil Palm	3	2	1.20
	Sugarcane	4	2	1.00
Horticulture	Passion Fruit	5	3	1.20
	Grape	5	3	1.20
	M. Orange	5	3	1.00
	Aloe Vera	4	2	1.00
	Chayote	4	2	1.00
	Pineapple	4	2	1.00
	Arecanut	5	3	1.00
	Tung	4	2	1.00
AH &Vety	Dairy	3	2	1.25
	Layer	3	2	1.00
	Broiler	3	2	1.00
	Piggery	3	2	1.00
	Mithun	3	2	1.00
Fisheries	Aqua Culture	3	2	1.00
	Polyculture	3	2	1.00
Soil & Water Conservation	Rubber	7	4	1.00
	Broom	4	3	0.88
	Coffee	7	4	0.88
Sericulture	Mulberry	4	2	1.00
Forest	Bamboo	9	5	1.00

Source: www.nlup.mizoram.gov.in, Accessed on 26.02.2013 @ 8PM

cent of the total amount. Thus, average of 30 per cent of the assistance to the beneficiaries could be delivered to the beneficiaries by the end of the first year. Meanwhile, almost 70 per cent (69 per cent and 67 per cent) was given to the beneficiaries within one and a half year, i.e. after the third instalment. Thus, the case of horticulture sector indicates a smooth process in the delivery of assistance to the beneficiaries and no major deviation from the notified Calendar of Works was observed.

Table 7.10
Abstract of the Release of NLUP Assistance under Industrial Sector

Sl. No.	Trade/Activities	No. of Instalment	Coverage (Year)	Total Assistance (Rs. In lakh)
1.	Auto Rick Shaw Service	1	1	1.16
2.	Automobile Works	3	2	1.00
3.	Bakery	3	2	1.00
4	Beauty Parlour	3	2	1.00
5.	Blacksmithy	3	2	1.00
6.	Broom Making-I	3	2	1.00
7.	Broom Making-II	2	1	1.00
8.	Cane & Bamboo Works	3	2	1.00
9.	Carpentry & Wood Processing-I	2	2	1.05
10.	Carpentry & Wood Processing-II	2	2	1.05
11.	Chow Making	3	2	1.00
12.	Desktop Publishing	1	1	1.00
13.	Electronic Repairing Works	3	2	1.00
14.	Hair Cutting	3	2	1.00
15.	Handloom	3	2	1.00
16.	Knitting	3	2	1.00
17.	Leather & Hood works, and Shoe Repairing	3	2	1.00
18.	Petty Trade-I (Grocery Shop)	3	2	1.00
19.	Petty Trade-II (Vegetable Shop)	2	1	0.50
20.	Petty Trade-III (Tea Stall)	2	1	0.50
21.	Petty Trade-IV (Wayside Food Stall)	3	2	0.80
22.	Photography & Videography	1	1	1.00
23.	Rice Hulling Works	3	2	1.00
24.	Shoe Repairing (Home Base)	2	1	0.50
25.	Square Agarbati Stick Making-I	3	2	1.00
26.	Square Agarbati Stick Making-II	2	1	0.50
27.	Steel Fabrication	3	2	1.00
28.	Tailoring	3	2	1.00
29.	Tinsmithy	3	2	1.00

Source: Industries Department, Government of Mizoram, 'Model Schemes of NLUP', 2011.

The detailed breakup of expenditure for assistance to beneficiaries under horticulture sector is presented in Table 7.12. With the exception of GI Wires and planting materials for some crops, the beneficiaries were given cash assistance. It was left to the beneficiaries to collect the materials needed for their trades by using their cash assistance. If the family members do not

Table 7.11
Periodic Flow of Input Supplies to the NLUP beneficiaries—A case of Horticulture (1st Phase)

Trade	*Year*	*Instalment*	*Period*	*Amount (Rs.)*	*Cumulative (Rs.)*	*Cumulative (%)*
Passion Fruit	1st Yr. (2010)	1st	Oct - Dec	20000	20000	16.67
	1st Yr. (2011)	2nd	Jan - Mar	14500	34500	28.75
	2nd Yr.(2011)	3rd	Apr-Sept	52400	86900	72.42
	2nd Yr.(2011)	4th	Oct-mar	18100	105000	87.5
	3rd Yr.(2012)	5th	Apr-Sept	15000	120000	100
Grape	1st Yr. (2010)	1st	Oct-Dec	15000	15000	12.5
	1st Yr. (2011)	2nd	Jan-Mar	20000	35000	29.17
	2nd Yr.(2011)	3rd	Apr-Sept	55500	90500	75.42
	2nd Yr.(2011)	4th	Oct-mar	14500	105000	87.5
	3rd Yr.(2012)	5th	Apr-Sept	15000	120000	100
M. Orange	1st Yr. (2010)	1st	Oct-Dec	15000	15000	15
	1st Yr. (2011)	2nd	Jan - Mar	12500	27500	27.5
	2nd Yr.(2011)	3rd	Apr-Sept	43936	71436	71.44
	2nd Yr.(2011)	4th	Oct-mar	16564	88000	88
	3rd Yr.(2012)	5th	Apr-Sept	12000	100000	100
Aloe Vera	1st Yr. (2010)	1st	Oct-Dec	10000	10000	10
	1st Yr. (2011)	2nd	Jan-Mar	10000	20000	20
	2nd Yr.(2011)	3rd	Apr-Sept	50500	70500	70.5
	2nd Yr.(2011)	4th	Oct-mar	29500	100000	100
Chayote	1st Yr. (2010)	1st	Oct - Dec	11400	11400	13.4
	1st Yr. (2011)	2nd	Jan-Mar	3500	14900	17.51
	2nd Yr.(2011)	3rd	Apr-Sept	51600	51600	60.63
	2nd Yr.(2011)	4th	Oct-mar	33500	85100	100
Pineapple	1st Yr. (2010)	1st	Oct - Dec	11000	11000	11
	1st Yr. (2011)	2nd	Jan-Mar	22500	33500	33.5
	2nd Yr.(2011)	3rd	Apr-Sept	37396	70896	70.9
	2nd Yr.(2011)	4th	Oct-mar	29104	100000	100
Arecanut	1st Yr. (2010)	1st	Oct - Dec	10000	10000	10
	1st Yr. (2011)	2nd	Jan-Mar	23000	33000	33
	2nd Yr.(2011)	3rd	Apr-Sept	25548	58548	58.55
	2nd Yr.(2011)	4th	Oct-mar	24464	83012	83.01
	3rd Yr.(2012)	5th	Apr-Sept	16988	100000	100
Tung	1st Yr. (2010)	1st	Oct - Dec	14200	14200	14.2
	1st Yr. (2011)	2nd	Jan-Mar	35800	50000	50
	2nd Yr.(2011)	3rd	Apr-Sept	15112	65112	65.11
	2nd Yr.(2011)	4th	Oct-mar	34888	100000	100

Source: www.nlup.mizoram.gov.in, Accessed on 26.02.2013 @ 9pm

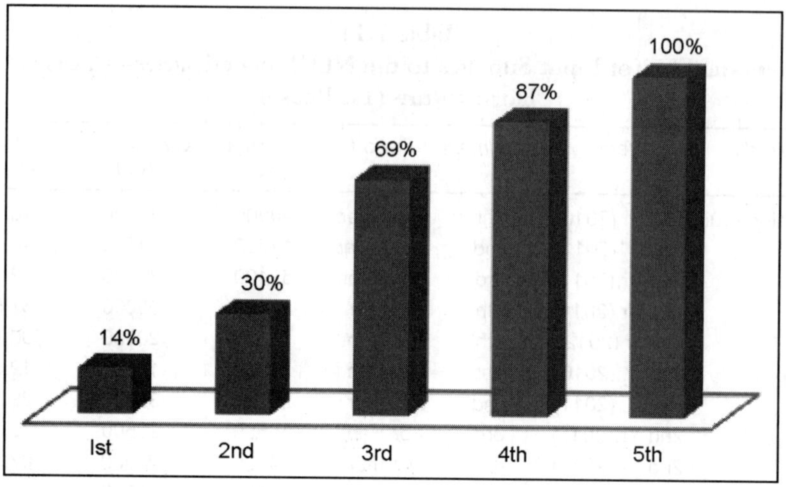

Fig. 7.3: Comulative Achievement of Assistance under Horticulture Sector (Ist Phase)-Trades having 5 instalments

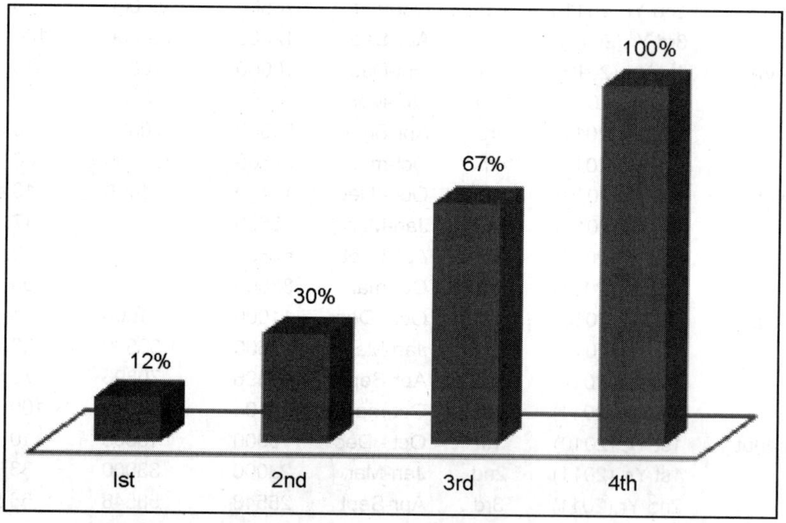

Fig. 7.4: Comulative Achievement of Assistance under Horticulture Sector (Ist Phase)-Trades having 4 instalments

want to hire outside labour but want to do the work on their own, the cash assistance could be used to meet the family consumption needs. Families cultivating tung were allowed to adopt intercropping in their field by

Table 7.12
Detailed Breakup of the Input supply to the NLUP beneficiaries—A Case of Horticulture

Sl. No.	Head of Assistance	Rate of Assistance per Beneficiary (Rs.)								
		M. Orange	Grape	Tung	Tea	Aloe Vera	Arecanut	Pineapple	Chayote	Passion Fruit
1.	Land Preparation	10,000	5,600	13,200	25,650	7,000	15,000	16,900	9,900	–
2.	Wooden Post	–	24,400	–	–	–	–	–	7,260	23,600
3.	Manures and Fertilizers	5,000	3,450	5,000	10,000	6,900	9,000	11,000	7,040	5,000
4.	Farm House	10,000	7,500	7,500	–	7,500	11,500	7,500	14,900	8,100
5.	G.I. Wire	–	47,600	–	–	–	–	–	35,100	48,300
6.	Rain Water Harvesting	15,000	15,000	15,000	–	18,540	15,000	15,000	15,000	15,000
7.	Half Moon Terracing	12,500	–	–	–	–	30,000	–	5,000	–
8.	Planting Materials	40,000	5,000	400	44,000	30,600	12,000	43,100	500	–
9.	Tools and Implements	–	2,000	2,000	2,750	710	2,000	2,000	2,000	3,000
10.	Transportation	2,500	1,550	2,500	2,550	3,750	2,500	2,500	1,800	1,500
11.	P.P. Measures	5,000	1,000	1,000	2,050	7,500	3,000	2,000	1,500	1,800
12.	Angle Iron Post	–	6,900	–	–	–	–	–	–	12,700
13.	Cost Gingerseed Rhizome	–	–	16,900	–	–	–	–	–	–
14.	Ginger Harvesting	–	–	6,500	–	–	–	–	–	–
15.	Sowing Seed Rhizome	–	–	30,000	–	–	–	–	–	–
16.	Catering young trees	–	–	–	10,000	–	–	–	–	–
17.	Shade Management	–	–	–	3,000	–	–	–	–	–
18.	Earthing Up	–	–	–	–	17,500	–	–	–	–
19.	Seedlings	–	–	–	–	–	–	–	–	1,000
	Total	**100000**	**120000**	**100000**	**100000**	**100000**	**100000**	**100000**	**100000**	**120000**

Source: Directorate of Horticulture, Flow of Material Supplies, Letter No.B.13014/18/2012-DTE (HORT-NLUP) dated 01.02.2013.

cultivating ginger in addition to the main crop. Further, for the beneficiaries cultivating crops like mandarin orange, areca nut, etc. who were supplied seedlings by the department through the approved suppliers, the amount required for the procurement of seedlings were deducted from their cash assistance.

As per the record of NIB, there were 18 trades in which material assistance was given by the concerned line department. The list of such trades along with the details of material provided and its share in the total assistance is given in Table 7.13. Beneficiaries adopting horticulture trades were given GI Wire as material assistance equivalent to Rs. 47,600 which is around 35-40 per cent of the total assistance. Soil and Water Conservation Department also supplied seedlings for beneficiaries adopting rubber and coffee plantation which are 24 per cent and 16.48 per cent of the total assistance respectively. It was the AH & Vety Department that provided material assistance for all trades under it with their percentage share in the total assistance being 76.68 per cent for dairy, 24 per cent for piggery, 80 per cent for mithun, and 10 per cent for poultry farming. At the same time, Industries Department also provided machines for six trades that had percentage share ranging from 40 per cent to 100 per cent.

The percentage share of the material assistance is lowest in case of poultry (10 per cent) where beneficiaries were given chicks. This is followed by coffee trade (16.48 per cent) where the beneficiaries were supplied seedlings only; and further is followed by bamboo (17.20 per cent) where seedlings and water tanks were provided. The material supply percentage is highest in case of Auto Rickshaw where the beneficiaries were provided the vehicle in complete form including registration and insurance fees. This is followed by Carpentry and Wood Processing II where machine (VBS-24) was provided which is equivalent to 82.86 per cent of the total assistance. To sum up, beneficiaries of NLUP were given not only the cash assistance, but also substantial amount in the form of materials required for the activities.

7.7. Infrastructure Development under NLUP

As explained earlier, the main aim of the NLUP Convergence scheme is creation of infrastructure through the funding of CSS. The scheme is like a host that mobilises funds from different sources for the creation of necessary infrastructures so that there is no duplication of work. The infrastructures

Table 7.13
Contribution of Material/Kind Assistances under NLUP (as on February 2013)

Sl. No.	*Trade*	*Department (Sector)*	*Material Provided*	*Total Assistance (Rs.)*	*Value of Material Assistance (Rs.)*	*Material Assistance (%)*
1.	Grape Cultivation	Horticulture	G.I. Wire	1,20,000	47,600	39.67
2.	Chayote	Horticulture	G.I. Wire	1,00,000	35,100	35.10
3.	Passion Fruit	Horticulture	G.I. Wire	1,20,000	48,300	40.25
4.	Semi-Intensive Aqua Culture	Fisheries	Urea, MOP, Fish Feed, etc	44,000	13,858	31.50
5.	Silkworm Rearing	Sericulture	GCI Sheet, Rearing Net	1,00,000	19,167	19.17
6.	Dairy Farming	AH &Vety	Cows, insurance	1,25,000	95,850	76.68
7.	Pig Farming	AH &Vety	Piglets	1,00,000	24,000	24.00
8.	Mithun Farming	AH &Vety	Mithun	1,00,000	80,000	80.00
9.	Poultry Farming	AH &Vety	Chicks	1,00,000	10,000	10.00
10.	Rubber Plantation	S & WC	Stump	1,00,000	24,000	24.00
11.	Coffee	S & WC	Seedlings	88,000	14,500	16.48
12.	Bamboo	Forest	Seedlings, Water tank	1,00,000	17,200	17.20
13.	Auto-Rickshaw	Industries	Auto-Rickshaw	1,16,000	1,16,000	100.00
14.	Carpentry & Wood Processing-I	Industries	VBS-18	1,05,000	65,000	61.90
15.	Carpentry & Wood Processing-II	Industries	VBS-24	1,05,000	87,000	82.86
16.	Tailoring	Industries	TSD, Overlock, JM, etc	1,00,000	52,000	52.00
17.	Handloom	Industries	Zo-loom, etc	1,00,000	42,700	42.70
18.	Sq. Agarbati Stick Making	Industries	Machines	1,00,000	40,000	40.00

Source: Information submitted to OSD Monitoring Cell, NIB by NLUP Nodal Officers of Respective Line Departments, 2013.

that are developed will facilitate or help the NLUP beneficiaries directly or indirectly in undertaking their trades. It may be noted that whenever we talk about convergence of NLUP with the funding of several CSS, it does not necessarily mean that all funds required for such activities would be met from the CSS only. The fund obtained from other sources like ACA for NLUP would be combined with the CSS funds. Sometimes, the contributions made from the NLUP fund were used as matching share requirements for central funding sources. As per the record of the NIB, as much as Rs. 1,108 lakh of the NLUP fund was spent till August 2016 as matching contribution of CSS that converged with the programme.

The list of infrastructures developed under the scheme to improve the sustainability of the production and their respective expenditures is presented in Table 7.14. It is shown that a sum of Rs. 185 lakh was spent for infrastructure development in the agriculture sector basically for quality control and capacity development. It established comprehensive laboratory centre for soil testing, seeds, etc. near the Directorate of Agriculture Office at Aizawl at the cost of Rs. 150 lakh, and Integrated Training Centre (ITC) was also upgraded with a total expenditure of Rs. 35 lakh.

Table 7.14
Material Infrastructure Developed under NLUP Convergence Scheme

Sl. No.	*Department*	*Infrastructure Developed*	*Expenditure (Rs. In lakh)*
1.	Agriculture	i) Establishment of Laboratory Centre	150.00
		ii) Upgradation of Integrated Training Centre	35.00
2.	Horticulture	Establishment of Multi-crop Nursery	100.00
3.	S & WC	Establishment of Coffee & Rubber Nurseries	40.00
4.	AH &Vety	Piglets Multiplication Centre, Poultry Development, etc	442.00
5.	Fisheries	Construction and Renovation of hatcheries	24.05
6.	Sericulture	Construction of Rearing House & Grainage	150.00
	Total		**941.05**

Source: NLUP Implementing Board, Government of Mizoram. Dated 18.8.2016.

In view of the demand-supply gap for planting materials of horticulture crops like orange, areca nut, etc., the Horticulture Department took initiative by instituting a project called multi-crop nursery where the local entrepreneurs and farmers were given interest-free loan for the establishment of nurseries. A sum of Rs. 100 lakh was spent for this initiative. It was reported that almost 100 per cent of the planting materials required by the 3rd and 4th Phase beneficiaries could be met from these nurseries. At the same time, raising of rubber and coffee seeds require technology that cannot be undertaken easily. Recognising this fact, the Soil and Water Conservation Department (S&WC) took initiative by spending Rs. 40 lakh. It established coffee nurseries in Aizawl, Kolasib, Khawzawl, Hriphaw, Mamit, Thenzawl, Thaizawl, Hnahthial, and Sihtlangpui; and rubber nurseries in Borai, Hortoki, Rangte, and Chhungkhum. Similarly, Sericulture Department also constructed rearing house at Champhai, Rotlang E, Zobawk, and a cold storage at Zemabawk. AH & Vety Department also established piglet multiplication centre at Aizawl, while Fisheries Department constructed new hatcheries and renovated the existing one with an expenditure of Rs. 24.05 lakh.

The initiatives for infrastructure development under NLUP were normally meant for enhancement of quality and production capacity of seed/input supplies for the farmers. The problem faced by the farmers in the state since long time back is the unavailability of quality seeds and planting materials. They have to depend on the traders from other states who would bring in materials whose quality is unknown. This led to farmers' distress as these traders brought inferior ones in many cases. Similarly, as the local product is extremely insufficient to meet the local demand, the farmers have no option but to depend on piglets imported from outside — from Myanmar and from other Indian states. However, movement of animals across the border is very risky due to frequent spread of diseases, which often cause huge loss to the farming population. Considering all these cases, it is highly necessary to enhance the capacity of producing seeds and planting materials for the livelihood security of the farming population in the long run. So, although the infrastructures developed under the NLUP Convergence Scheme are still insufficient to cater the need of the farmers, the cases that are focussed upon here points to the added requirements of the state.

While giving priority to the enhancement of production and input supply chain through the provision of necessary infrastructures, it is also necessary to take initiatives towards development of marketing infrastructures. The NLUP programme envisioned creation of congenial environment for the existence of efficient market channels for the produce of the beneficiaries by making physical and institutional infrastructures.

For this, a separate cell called NLUP Marketing Board was established at NIB. These infrastructures were created through convergence scheme of NLUP. It may be noted that it is the responsibility of the line departments to identify required infrastructure and prepare detailed proposals in their respective fields, and the NIB will coordinate the process and make fund allocation. The list of physical infrastructures developed under the programme, as obtained from NIB, is presented in Table 7.15.

Table 7.15
Development of Marketing Infrastructure under NLUP Convergence Scheme

Sl. No.	Marketing Infrastructures	Number	Amount (Rs. in lakh)
1.	Construction of Marketshed	4	43.00
2.	Multipurpose Godown (50 MT each)	6	57.50
3.	Storage House for Broom (50 MT each)	9	90.00
4.	Dairy Feed Godown (25 MT) at Muthi	1	5.00
5.	Orange Storage House (25 MT) at Leng	1	5.00
6.	Storage House for Squash (25 MT) at Nisapui	1	5.00
7.	Potential Area Connectivity/Link Road (260 Kms) @ Rs. 5 lakhs/Km	104	1300.00
8.	Construction and Improvement of Suspension Bridge for Agriculture Link Road	12	41.00
9.	Construction of Pack House	1	945.00
	Total	**139**	**2491.50**

Source: NLUP Implementing Board, Government of Mizoram, Dated 18.8.2016.

The State Government has commendable success in the construction of agriculture link road (Potential Area Connectivity) under the NLUP scheme. The main purpose of constructing link road is to connect all the potential areas by motor road to ensure easy accessibility. It constructed link roads of 260 km long in 104 locations with a total expenditure of Rs. 1,300 lakh. Substantial amount was also spent on renovation, maintenance, and improvement of the existing link roads. Further, an expenditure amounting to Rs. 41 lakh was also made for the improvement and construction of suspension bridges connecting the potential areas. Development of link road has the potential of having backward and forward linkages such as the enhancement of production activities and facilitation of marketing activities respectively. However, the requirements for regular maintenance of these roads to ensure all time access by vehicles would remain a major challenge. It is necessary to evolve mechanism for the maintenance of these roads with active involvement of the people or the stakeholder farmers.

A major initiative for market infrastructure development is the establishment of Pack House with a cost of Rs. 945 lakh at CEDAR Complex, Tuirial. The Pack House hosts activities like cleaning, sorting, grading, and cold storage for agricultural products like ginger, turmeric, orange, passion fruit, etc. The work has been started under the funding support of Agriculture Produce Export Development Agency (APEDA), Government of India. It is expected that all the items processed here would be made to meet the standard of export to other countries. The location is at the central part of the state which is around 40 km and 30 km from the Airport and the Rail Station (which is likely to be commissioned by 2019) respectively. The Pack House is expected to be one of the most important and significant market infrastructure developed under the NLUP.

Another initiative for the development of market infrastructure is construction of different types of storehouses (godowns) of different capacities. 18 storehouses (multipurpose for brooms, feeds, squash, and orange) were constructed at different places with a total expenditure of Rs. 162.5 lakh. In addition, four market sheds in Kolasib and Thenzawl, meatshops at Thenzawl, Khawlailung, and Khatla were constructed with a total expenditure of Rs. 43 lakh. These market sheds are meant for selling of the agricultural produce of the state in the local market.

7.8. Captive Farming

One attractive initiative undertaken under NLUP is Captive Farming of Passion Fruit (CFPF) through the convergence scheme of NLUP and Rashtriya Krishi Vikas Yojana (RKVY), a centrally sponsored scheme. This captive farming can be considered as contract farming where the farmers are provided the inputs by a sponsor agency with a commitment to purchase their products. Against the problem of the fruit processing plants operated by a public sector enterprise called Mizoram Food and Allied Industries Corporation Ltd. (MIFCO) at Chhingchhip which could not run at its full capacity due to insufficiency of raw materials, the state government decided to introduce passion fruit cultivation in Tuikum Cluster, which is in the vicinity of this fruit processing plant to be taken up under Captive Farming system. Input requirements equivalent to Rs. 1.2 lakh was to be provided to the 500 selected farmers in this Cluster, and the produce of the farmers would be purchased by the MIFCO for processing and its further marketing.

As per the record of the NIB, the total project cost is Rs. 783.62 lakh, of which Rs. 262.50 lakh was to be met from RKVY fund while the remaining amount of Rs. 521.12 lakh would be given from NLUP scheme. The beneficiaries were provided cash assistance for land development and construction of farm house, while assistance in kind was given in the form of seedlings and farming equipments. While the role of the state government was to provide cash and material assistance to the beneficiaries, the actual execution was to be undertaken by MIFCO and village level committees for this particular crop. The government also provided funding support to MIFCO for procurement of the fruits from the farmers. That is, the revolving fund would be provided by the government (NIB). Although an issue exists on how long this initiative would sustain, all the produce of the farmers, for the time being, would be procured by MIFCO and there will be no marketing problem for the farmers.

7.9. Collaboration with UN Agencies

Acting on the request of the State Government, the Food and Agriculture Organisation (FAO) entered Mizoram to supplement various livelihood activities under NLUP. In the meeting organised in New Delhi on 28 December 2012, the FAO deputed Expert Team members from the University of Minnesota in January 2013. Their recommendation was submitted to the Planning Commission and the International Headquarters of FAO. As a result, the Expert Team of various agencies of United Nations Organisation (UNO) viz., FAO, UNDP, UNIDO, IFAD, and ILO visited Mizoram during January 2014 which culminated in the launching of 'Joint UN Initiative in Mizoram' on 16th October, 2014. Based on this decision, an Expert Team called 'Technical Team' was constituted to prepare a project for Mizoram with certain specific objectives, namely, food security, livelihood security, environmental security and energy security. Barring 'energy security', the other items are the primary objectives of NLUP.

The programme components of the UN Joint Initiative encompassed the following components:

(i) Identification of bio-diversity rich and ecologically sensitive regions.
(ii) Use and preservation of indigenous knowledge.
(iii) Analysis of shifting agriculture patterns and local ecosystem.
(iv) Promotion of responsible use and maintenance of natural resources in high priority areas.
(v) Assessment of markets for horticulture, handicraft products and opportunities for women and local youth to promote and manage community operated and natural resource based enterprises in a sustainable manner.
(vi) Assessment of employment opportunities for local youth, training and skill development to increase livelihood opportunities for the youth and rural population.
(vii) Provision of vocational training and skill development through the National Rural Livelihood Mission and other key national skill initiatives, and
(viii) Development and improvement of processing and production based on locally available sources and technology.

The 'Technical Team' in consultation with the Government and NGOs, farmers, etc. decided to list specific activities to be undertaken for the period 2014-17. The following activities were identified for operation under the Joint UN Initiative:

1. Prepare project for Joint UN Programme for ecosystem management including bamboo forest.
2. Three districts, namely Mamit, Kolasib, and Lunglei, were selected as pilot district for demonstration of sustainable intensification of high value horticultural crops.
3. Two districts, namely Serchhip and Aizawl, have been selected as pilot districts for demonstration of sustainable intensification of high value horticultural crops.
4. Facilitate maintenance of select priority roads under ILO as per existing model.
5. Provide technical assistance to the Mizoram State Skill Development Mission to improve supply chains.
6. Initiate pilot projects to develop value chain for bamboo production.
7. Initiate pilot project to improve value chain for horticultural crops including ginger, turmeric, and aloe vera.

8. To provide technical and other strategic support for trans-boundary risks including animal diseases, plant pests especially in the context of control of major animal diseases and plant pests.
9. Support capacity building and provide training to assess the environmental impacts of displacement on ecosystem.
10. Facilitate training of trainers on "Start and Improve Your Business Programme".
11. Support an environmental impact assessment of link roads to improve value chain system.
12. Identify concrete steps that involve women at higher level in the value chain for bamboo and horticulture.
13. Energy related activities for processing and value addition.

Four UN Agencies namely UNDP, FAO, ILO and UNIDO participated in the initiatives and have started operation in their respective fields. The UNDP was tasked with the role of coordination among the participating agencies, and had established Office in the office premises of Directorate of AH & Vety. In its attempt to improve the agricultural value chain and marketing channels, the UNDP deputed Market Consultant who would be assisted by a team of 'Marketing Task Force'. In addition to the enhancement of agricultural marketing scenario, the agency also took initiative for capacity development to enhance the input supply chain management in Mizoram.

In 2014, the FAO signed an agreement with the State Government to try and address the problem of the livestock industry, especially piggery sector that had been frequented by Porcine Reproductive Respiratory Syndrome (PRRS) since 2012. As per the agreement, the FAO prepared and submitted, in 2015, the Comprehensive Guidelines to Control and Contain PRRS. Under the joint funding support of the State government and this agency, action is underway to control and contain PRRS that had caused huge loss to the farmers multiple times. In addition, it also initiated Farmers' Field School (FFS) that had helped the farmers in farming activities. An initiative undertaken alongside the FFS is the development of Mizoram Slope Agriculture Land Technology (MiSALT) where local technology of soil protection, called *Changkham,* in shifting cultivation was integrated with an improved and sustainable method. Though it is too early to make comment on the success or failure of these initiatives, there have been some signs of successes on it.

ILO also conducted Comprehensive Survey on the existing scenario of employment, unemployment, underemployment, etc. to identify skill development needs, or skill gap, so as to evolve proper manpower planning policy in the state. It may be noted that Mizoram has vast bamboo resources that has not been utilised in a meaningful way except for local needs. To leverage the potential of this huge untapped bamboo resource, UNIDO had taken up initiatives to enhance bamboo value chain for promotion of livelihood. For this, Comprehensive Bamboo Project is being prepared by this agency. The success of this project would bring huge employment opportunities for people in the bamboo related livelihood activities.

7.10. Concluding Note

The New Land Use Policy implemented in Mizoram since the financial year 2010-11 has given strong impetus for the transformation of the state economy whereby the shifting cultivators would be settled in more sustainable means of livelihood. The total approved amount of Rs. 2,873.13 crore, for a physical target of 1.2 lakh families to be covered in five years, is a substantial amount for the state with population of around 11 lakh and total annual budget of about Rs. 7,000 crore. It is the biggest project ever introduced in the state specifically meant for the upliftment of the poor households. The State Government showed coordinated effort in its implementation by bringing into the bandwagon several governmental departments that are involved in developmental works. The government has recorded commendable achievement in the implementation of NLUP in terms of physical target where it significantly exceeded the original target, and financial achievement as it could achieve expenditure of more than half of the total approved amount within a span of five years. Considering the total number of households in the Population Census 2011, NLUP has covered 59.25 per cent of the total number of households in the state. As it encompassed a wide range of activities with a provision of creating necessary infrastructure, it may be reasonable to say that the length and breadth of the coverage of the scheme is tremendous.

Further, the assistance to the beneficiaries, whose crops are on gestation, through livelihood promotion activities is essential for successful harvesting of their crops, while those on the verge of harvesting their crops also needs assistance for marketing of their produce. In view of this, the State Government in collaboration with some UN Agencies launched joint initiatives with proposed field of operation. This is in line with the requirements of the NLUP beneficiaries. Though the initiative is only at its initial stage, it is clear that State Government can be considered successful in achieving its flagship NLUP programme global recognition and participation of international agencies towards the development of the state.

The project period was supposed to be completed by the end of 2014-15 financial year as per the allocation made by the then Planning Commission. However, only 61.11 per cent of the total approved amount could be achieved till May 2016 leaving around 40 per cent unspent even after completion of five years of its implementation. This clearly indicates the situation where the smooth progress of the scheme is being hampered by technical inefficiency in the delivery system. The assistances were to be delivered as per the Calendar of Work which demands regular activities on the part of the beneficiaries as well as the line departments. Meanwhile, some departments are overloaded as the physical achievements were extremely higher than the targeted. They cannot be accommodated easily by the existing strength and capacity of the departments.

Deviation of the physical achievements from its target should be an area of concern as it can adversely affect the successful implementation of the scheme. Physical targets were determined for each sector in view of the various factors like availability of resources, marketing opportunities, etc. Achievement of the desired physical target as set out in the DPR would have implication towards the achievement of the targeted sustainable land use pattern. However, the physical achievements showed significant deviations from these physical targets. While the two key land based sectors, namely agriculture and horticulture, were targeted to contribute 50.33 per cent; only 33.11 per cent adopted these trades, thus showing a deviation by more than 17 per cent. Similarly, while the target for industries sector was only 5.42 per cent, the physical achievement was more than 22 per cent. The percentage achieved by AH & Vety sector was 28.06 per cent of the total number of beneficiaries, which is 12.34 per cent higher than its target. This structural aberration of physical achievement may adversely affect the success of the scheme in the long run.

The tendency of the beneficiaries to choose trades with higher amount of assistance and those that can be easily taken up, is unbecoming as it can easily invite criticism from outside the government. The unduly higher number of beneficiaries adopting poultry, piggery, and petty trade also implicates such problem. These trades can be easily taken up, but it is very difficult to monitor their progress and requires continuity and entrepreneurial skills on the part of the beneficiaries which cannot be expected to come by easily. These beneficiaries can stop their activities any time due to one reason or the other, thereby defaming the name of the programme.

The progress of the implementation, and fund flow of CSS for NLUP Convergence Schemes was very slow. The overall achievement of convergence scheme for development and infrastructure components are 57.57 per cent and 53.01 per cent respectively. Further, the way in which the convergence scheme for infrastructure development was handled was quite non-transparent and there was no effective mechanism to involve grassroots stakeholders. As huge amount of expenditure had already been disbursed for beneficiary assistance, it is necessary to show utmost effort in the creation of necessary infrastructures. They are essential for facilitating further production and marketing of the produce of the beneficiaries which would start in the near future. The Captive Farming System for passion fruit is one innovative initiative undertaken through NLUP for the emergence of organised agricultural marketing system. However, its sustainability in the long run is highly questionable given the existing level of management and operational efficiency of MIFCO. Such a big push may be beyond its capacity in terms of management and marketing strategy.

8

REVIEW OF NLUP 2011

8.1. Background

Shifting cultivation (jhumming) is universally agreed as a primitive and unproductive method of cultivation (Garbyal, 1999) and so, its control becomes imperative, which would not only improve the ecological quality but also enhance crop productivity (Sati and Rinawma, 2014). The main objective of all land use policies adopted in Mizoram in the past was to abolish the practice of shifting cultivation by introducing settled cultivation. 'Garden Colony' project implemented in 1978, 'Jhum Control Policy' (JCP) in 1987, and 'Mizoram Intodelhna Project' (MIP) in 2002 were all meant to shift the jhumia families away to settled cultivation. They were introduced on pilot basis for selected crops in selected development blocks, and the beneficiaries were given assistance in the form of cash and materials. However, these projects could not make much headway mostly due to fund limitation and political setback of the parties that introduced the policies. The scope of the MIP was slightly wider than the others as it envisioned creation of necessary infrastructures like link roads, cold storages, etc. But the project suffered strong public criticism over the poor delivery of assistance and lack of effective monitoring system, and the frequent changes in the Policy Guidelines to accommodate vested interests. Consequently, the policy could not be implemented in a meaningful way even before the change in ministry.

Unlike the other land use projects, the New Land Use Policy (NLUP) was implemented three times in Mizoram (1984, 1991, and 2011) under the political leadership of Shri Lal Thanhawla of Indian National Congress party. The number of families covered and benefit packages under NLUP in each of these phases were larger than the other projects. The number of families covered were 15076, 49025, and 120000 in its First Round (1984-85 to 1986-87), Second Round (1990-91 to 1996-97), and Third Round (2010-11 to 2014-15) respectively. The first two rounds were restricted to rural areas with specific target to control jhum cultivation, while the third round covered both rural and urban areas. Although the main objective was to abandon the practice of shifting cultivation in rural areas, the third round of NLUP also covered poor households that do not have sustainable livelihoods. Thus, the project worked to stop jhum cultivation and to improve the livelihood security of the poor households by providing specific activities that are suitable for them.

The NLUP 2011 was implemented in the form of a four tier management system, and the line departments took the responsibility of need assessment and delivery of assistances to the beneficiaries. Unlike the previous rounds of NLUP where the project was coordinated by Rural Development Department, NLUP Implementing Board was constituted to be the executing agency that coordinates the activities undertaken at different levels of project management. The project fund was clearly divided into three major components, viz. development, infrastructure, and management. The development component is primarily meant for beneficiary assistance which constituted around 90 per cent of the total expenditure. At the same time, the policy introduced convergence scheme where various related centrally sponsored schemes (CSS) were converged. Considerable amount was spent under this scheme, especially for infrastructure development. Another area that merits attention is the international recognition of this programme through the collaboration with UN Agencies. The state government and four agencies, namely UNDP, UNIDO, FAO, and ILO, launched 'Joint Initiative in Mizoram' on 16 October 2015 for food security, livelihood security, environmental security, and energy security which are mostly the core objectives of NLUP.

Given this background, it is considered necessary to review the implementation of the project and its immediate impacts, although it may be too early for it to have significant impacts on the economy. The review is divided into three broad areas — its impact on the macro-economy of the state, beneficiary performances, and the various dimensions of implementation of the programme. Required data were obtained from various sources like Directorate of Agriculture, Economics and Statistics, Planning and Programme Implementation, reports of the NLUP evaluation, etc. At the same time, primary data was collected by visiting five villages where the programme was implemented.

8.2. Macroeconomic View

8.2.1. Decrease in Jhum Area

Right from its inception, the main objective of NLUP was to put an end to the age old practice of shifting cultivation in Mizoram. So, the key parameter for the success of the scheme would be decrease in jhum area. To examine if the programme has impact on shifting cultivation practices in Mizoram as indicated by its area, the relevant information derived from the record of Directorate of Agriculture and Economic Survey, Department of Planning and Programme Implementation, Government of Mizoram were analysed. In addition to the analysis on the decline in absolute areas, attempt was also made to take into account the population increase to have a clearer view on the existing trend of declining jhum cultivation. The general trends of area under shifting cultivation (in hectares) and estimated area per person (in acres) are presented in Figures 8.1 and 8.2, respectively.

It can be observed from Figure 8.1 that the total jhum area decreased significantly from 55265 hectares in 1980-81 to 20064 hectares in 2014-15 at an annual compound rate of decrease of –1.5 per cent. To examine it further, the trend is divided into three stages — stage-1 (1980-81 to 1990-91), stage-2 (1990-91 to 2007-08), and stage-3 (2007-08 to 2014-15). Jhum area decreased by 33.56 per cent in stage-1 from 55265 hectares to 36716 hectares, while it increased by 22.42 per cent in stage-2 to 44947 hectares. Clear turn of the trend can be observed in stage-3 (after 2007-08) when jhum area decreased consistently from 44947 hectares in 2007-08 to 20064 hectares in 2014-15. The overall decline turns out to be 55.36 per cent. As this stage coincides with the NLUP, which was revived by the Congress Ministry after the General Election in 2008, it is safe to assume that jhumming had significantly decreased in Mizoram after the implementation of NLUP. Even though jhumming is not yet abandoned in the state as desired by the policy, its scale of operation reduced drastically after the implementation of NLUP. This can be one important case indicating the success of the programme in achieving its objective.

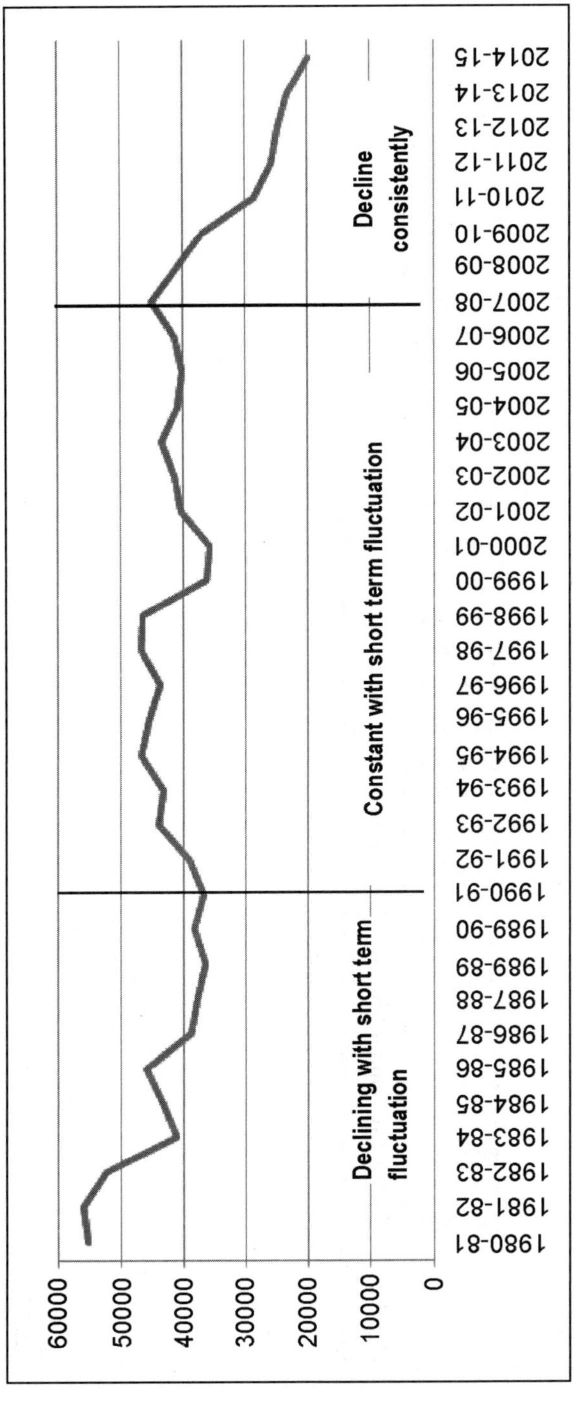

Fig. 8.1: Trend of Area under Shifting Cultivation in Mizoram (Hectares)
Source: Directorate of Agriculture & Economic Surveys (Various Issues), Mizoram

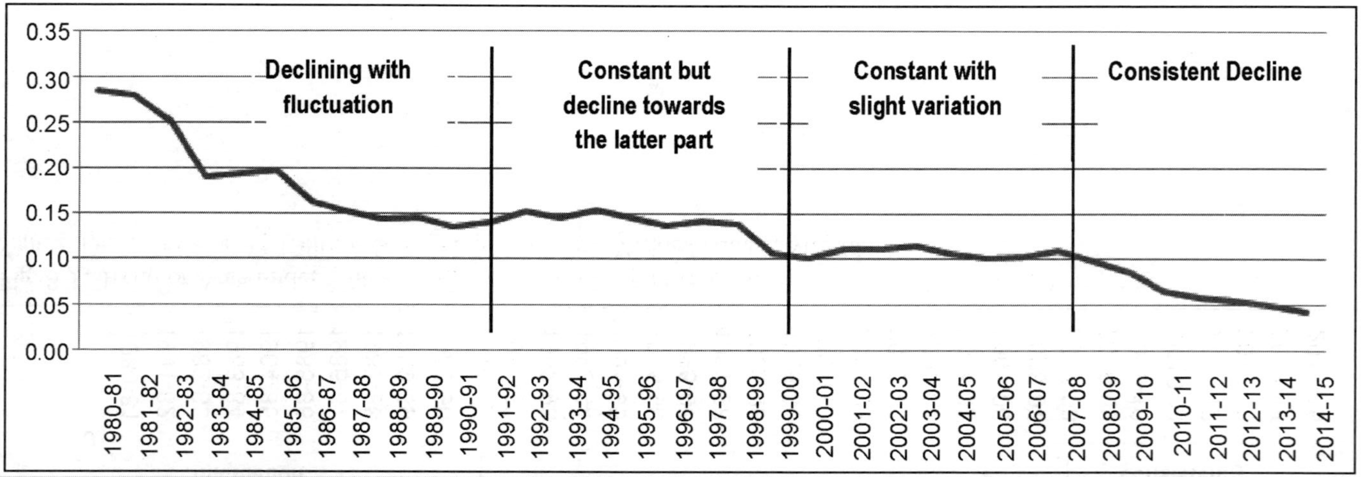

Fig. 8.2: Declining Area under Shifting Cultivation per Persons in Mizoram (in Acre)
Source: Directorate of Agriculture & Economic Surveys (Various Issues), Mizoram

To have more clarity on the decrease in jhum cultivation, further attempt was made to study the trend of area under jhum cultivation per person in the state. This is worked out by dividing the total jhum area by the projected population in a year based on the Population Census (given in the Table A4 in Appendix). This is presented in Figure 8.2. It can be observed that jhum area per person decreased continuously at Compound Annual Growth Rate (CAGR) of 3.99 per cent. Except for the period starting from 1999-00 to 2007-08 where a more or less constant trend was experienced, jhum area per person decreased in all the periods continuously. It decreased by 52.65 per cent between 1980-81 and 1990-91, and by 21.97 per cent between 1990-91 and 2007-08. The highest rate of decrease of jhum area per person was observed in the period after 2007-08 till 2014-15, which is more than 60 per cent. So, this is in support of the hypothesis that jhum cultivation decreased significantly after NLUP. The Consultative Committee for NLUP (CCN) in its study 'On the Success and Impact of NLUP under Horticulture Sector in Mizoram, 2015' observed that the average jhum size per family among the beneficiaries of the First and Second Phases (i.e. beneficiaries selected in the year 2010-11 and 2012-13) decreased by 22.52 per cent. Taking all these trends into account, it is clear that people had shifted away from jhum cultivation after the implementation of NLUP in Mizoram since 2010-11.

8.2.2. Impacts on Agriculture and Allied Sector

To examine the impact of NLUP on the growth of agriculture and allied activities covered by the programme during the pre- and post-project period, the data published by Directorate of Economics and Statistics in its 'Statistical Abstract of Mizoram: 2015' was adopted. The study decided to adopt this data because the Economics and Statistics Department has followed the same methodology of data collection for a very long time, and no alteration was mentioned in the report. The analysis used 2009-10 data as reference year as this is the latest year prior to the implementation of the project. The result is presented in Table 8.1. The cases presented here are the trades of NLUP, but it should be noted that this data represents the whole state, including NLUP beneficiaries as well as those that are not. So, the effect of natural growth (i.e. rate of growth which would be achieved even if the project was not implemented) cannot be ruled out while making

Table 8.1
Changes in the Key Indicators of Land Based Activities after NLUP in Mizoram

Sl. No.	*Activities/Crops*	*Unit*	*2009-10*	*2014-15*	*Change (%)*
1.	Sugarcane	Area (ha)	1434	1476	2.93
2.	Orange	Area (ha)	5348	14200	165.52
3.	Orange	Production (MT)	13265	41200	210.59
4.	Banana	Area (ha)	8660	10870	25.52
5.	Banana	Production (MT)	84810	141000	66.25
6.	Grape	Area (ha)	1232	2450	98.86
7.	Grape	Production (MT)	13736	22550	64.17
8.	Passion Fruit	Area (ha)	3150	980	-68.89
9.	Passion Fruit	Production (MT)	16411	2110	-87.14
10.	Squash (Chayote)	Area (ha)	2250	4800	113.33
11.	Squash (Chayote)	Production (MT)	34875	81390	133.38
12.	Arecanut	Area (Ha)	4800	10738	123.71
13.	Arecanut	Production (MT)	12390	7270	-41.32
14.	Wet Rice Cultivation	Area (ha)	10363	16866	62.75
15.	Oil Palm	Area (ha)	8261	20377	146.67
16.	Cow (Crossbred)	No.	6868	18722	172.60
17.	Milk	Production (MT)	10633	20495	92.75
18.	Fisheries	Area (Ha)	3953.8	4790	21.15
19.	Fish Production	Production (Qtl)	29160	59870	105.32
20.	Fish Seeds	No. (in lakh)	160	293	83.13
21.	Rubber	Area (ha)	426	821	92.72
22.	Mulberry	Production (MT)	60	351.24	485.40

Source: Directorate of Economics and Statistics, *Statistical Abstract of Mizoram: 2015*, Government of Mizoram.

comparison between the pre- and post-project period. For easy comprehension, the effect of natural growth may be arbitrarily set at 25 per cent, which is considered reasonable for a short span of five years. Further, some activities are yet to reach their full-grown stage and possibly bear maximum harvest, and thus, further increase can also be anticipated for such cases.

One conclusion that becomes very clear from Table 8.1 is that NLUP has positive impact in majority of the agriculture and allied activities considered in this table. The positive impact of NLUP can be seen in 16 out of the 22 cases considered even after taking into consideration the natural growth effect arbitrarily estimated at 25 per cent. It is commendable that production of silk (mulberry) increased by more than 400 per cent during this period and that production and area cover of orange increased by 210.59 per cent and 165.52 per cent respectively. The number of cows (crossbred) increased by 172.60 per cent, and milk production by 92.75 per cent. Areas and production of chayote (squash) increased by more than 100 per cent; and fish production also recorded an increase by more than 100 per cent during this period. Further, the increasing area of wet rice cultivation (WRC) by 62.73 per cent indicates the success of NLUP towards achieving one of its main objectives. Passion fruit, which was also promoted under MIP by the previous government, recorded a decrease in area and production. However, the recent initiative of Captive Farming system under NLUP is expected to have impact on passion fruit in the later years. Although areca nut needs around seven years in reaching its production stage, it recorded an area increase of more than 120 per cent. The decreasing production can be assumed to be the poor harvest of those planted prior to NLUP as the newly planted ones are yet to bear fruit. This clearly indicates the effect of NLUP on areca nut plantation. Given all these, it can be concluded that the NLUP implemented since 2010-11 has positively impacted the cultivation area and production of various agricultural and allied activities in Mizoram.

8.3. Beneficiary Performances

There are diverse areas of activities adopted as trades under NLUP, and thus, there cannot be a clear cut yardstick to measure the success of the beneficiaries. Even so, it is necessary to look into the performance of the beneficiaries to measure the success or failure of the programme. In the absence of a clear parameter to measure the performance of the beneficiaries, even in DPR and Calendar of Work, any method becomes subjective in nature and depends on the person who measures it. Whatever may be the case, it is necessary to measure it. To examine the performance of the beneficiaries, at least roughly, five villages namely Sihfa, Baktawng Tlangnuam, Bilkhawthlir South, Sekhum, and N. Mualcheng were visited. The required information was collected through interview and group discussion of knowledgeable persons in the village. The result is presented in Table 8.2. As no clear criterion was adopted in the process of data collection, the result presented in this table is completely based on the perception of the respondents and participants of the group discussion.

Table 8.2
Performance of Beneficiaries in the Selected Village (Summary Observations)

Trades	*M. Orange*	*Arecanut*	*Carpentry*	*Piggery*	*Poultry*	*Broom*	*WRC*	*Fisheries*	*Others*	*Total*
No. of Beneficiaries										
Sihfa	82	–	2	12	–	–	21	9	4	130
Baktawng T	17	–	88	11	8	52	1	–	55	232
Bilkhawthlir S	–	196	5	17	13	53	35	36	9	364
Sekhum	44	–	1	3	–	–	–	–	2	50
Total	143	196	96	43	21	105	57	45	70	776
Performing Beneficiaries (%)										
Sihfa	73.17	–	100	0	–	–	42.857	0	25	55.38
Baktawng T	0	–	100	0	0	0	0	–	45.45	48.71
Bilkhawthlir S	–	76.53	60	0	0	100	100	100	22.22	79.40
Sekhum	100	–	0	0	–	–	–	–	100	92.00
Combined	72.73	76.53	96.88	0	0	50.48	77.19	80	48.17	67.01
Non-Performing or Poorly Performed (%)										
Sihfa	24.39	–	0	100	–	–	42.86	100	75	40.77
Baktawng T	100	–	0	100	100	100	100	–	5.45	39.66
Bilkhawthlir S	–	23.47	40	100	100	0	0	0	0	23.08
Sekhum	0	–	100	100	–	–	–	–	0	8.00
Combined	25.87	23.47	3.13	100	100	49.52	17.54	20	8.57	30.03

Source: Field Visit, August 2016.

The number of beneficiaries considered in these exercises was not exhaustive, but they are expected to bear a clear picture on the trend of beneficiary performances. But first, the case of N. Mualcheng may be noted here. All the orange trees planted by 64 beneficiaries under NLUP were lost due to *citrus decline* (*serthlum tam*) which accounted for more than half of the beneficiaries in this village. Further, another 43 beneficiaries (34 per cent) who adopted WRC were found to be not working on their trade as is expected of them. So, the case of N. Mualcheng is not presented in Table 8.2.

It is entertaining to see from Table 8.2 that on an average, 67.01 per cent showed effort in their respective trades, while more than 30 per cent did not take any initiative in their trades for which they were given assistance(s). Even though the success level of these beneficiaries could not be clearly projected due to a number of reasons like crop loss due to disease, etc., it is encouraging to see more than half of the beneficiaries in these villages taking initiatives in their trades. The cases of two trades, piggery and poultry, under Animal Husbandry and Veterinary Department (AH & Vety) need attention. All the beneficiaries of these trades were non-performing and did not take initiatives in their trades. Although the people are well accustomed to livestock rearing, especially piggery and poultry, for domestic consumption, undertakings for commercial purposes require business and entrepreneurship skills which most Mizo lack. These trades had been included among the selected activities in several rural development and poverty alleviation schemes in the past. However, for them to become sustainable income sources is hardly seen in most of the cases. It is necessary to accept that government schemes in respect to AH & Vety trades like poultry, piggery, etc. are likely to fail in Mizoram, if not done on a large scale with clear managerial skills on the part of the beneficiaries.

Poor delivery of the assistance demoralised the beneficiaries which directly ramified their performance. Although as much as 73.17 per cent of the beneficiaries who adopted orange as their NLUP trade in Sihfa village had shown great enthusiasm by undertaking jungle clearance and land preparation, they started receiving materials (seeds) from the concerned line department only towards the end of the planting season of May to July. As it is certain that most plants would not survive even if they were planted once they arrived, the beneficiaries preferred to wait for next season. In the process, they lose enthusiasm to carry on with their trades, and thus, decided to take on their jhumming practice. This is in support to the observations of the Consultative Committee for NLUP (CCN) in its study on the 'Success and Impact of NLUP under Horticulture Sector in Mizoram: Mandarin Orange (2015)' which showed that 47.76 per cent of the beneficiaries received the seeds late. Meanwhile, Sekhum village which was awarded the 'Best Village under NLUP' in 2013 for their success in Orange trade is still going strong even after three years, as 100 per cent of the beneficiaries are still working on their trade. One of the factors for their success, as they claimed during the field exercise, was continuous monitoring of their progress by the concerned department and other stakeholders of the scheme as they adopted this village as a model village.

These cases clearly indicate the significance of active monitoring and efficient delivery of assistance as a main factor for the success of any scheme.

The performance of the beneficiaries under Industries Department was found to be very poor in urban areas, while the situation is slightly better in rural areas. This is shown by a study of the first and second phase beneficiaries conducted by Department of Economics, Mizoram University in 2015. Although the observations made by this study were based on the perception of the investigators about the performances of the beneficiaries they visited during the field exercise, their observations do indicate the performance of beneficiaries under Industries Department. Table 8.3 presents the results of this study.

Table 8.3
Investigators' Perception on the Performances of Beneficiaries under Industries Sector (%)

Sl. No	*Observations on the performances*	*Urban Areas*		*Rural Areas*	*Mizoram*
		Aizawl	*Other towns*		
1.	No Initiative or Non-performing	60.58	54.72	8.45	43.19
2.	Poorly Performing	13.37	7.49	25.30	15.33
3.	Performing	26.05	37.79	66.25	43.19

Source: Department of Economics (2015), *Survey and Impact Analysis of NLUP Beneficiaries* Mizoram University, 2015.

Table 8.3 clearly indicates mass failure of the scheme as 43.19 per cent of the beneficiaries did not take any initiative in their trades (i.e. non-performing), and another 15.33 per cent implemented it but only poorly. Thus, the success of NLUP under industries sector is not likely to be higher than 50 per cent as more than half of them were not functioning as desired. The situation is more acute in urban areas where more than 60 per cent and 54 per cent in Aizawl and other towns, respectively, were non-performing and did not take any initiative on their trade, though they were given the assistances. Including 'poorly performing' beneficiaries, 73.95 per cent and 62.21 per cent in Aizawl and other towns, respectively, were not working as required, and the remaining 26.05 per cent and 37.79 per cent only were working on their trades. As against this, the situation is comparatively better in rural areas where 66.25 per cent were found performing, and 25.30 per cent poorly performing; while only 8.45 per cent were non-performing beneficiaries.

To supplement the perception of the investigators, the respondent beneficiaries were asked to grade their level of success. In Aizawl city, 42.53 per cent admitted that they had failed in their trade, 25.72 per cent partially failed; and only 20.87 claimed to be successful and 10.88 per cent as partially successful. In the other towns, 53.02 per cent accepted that they failed (13.49 per cent partially failed and 39.53 per cent already failed). At the same time, the failed percentage is significantly lower in rural areas (villages) as 38.12 per cent failed (23.4 per cent partially failed and 14.72 per cent already failed). The poor performances of the beneficiaries according to the observations of the investigators were thus strongly supported by the beneficiaries' perceptions on their own performances.

The main reason for large scale failure in urban areas was the limited option given to the beneficiaries during their exercise of trade selection. Significant numbers of urban beneficiaries were not placed in trades of their choice but were allocated other trades. The urban poor, with limited technical and entrepreneurial skills, are not in a position to undertake skill-based activities that require working space. At the same time, trades with lesser skill requirement like piggery, poultry, etc. were not allowed in Aizawl city area, and consequently, large number of beneficiaries was practically obligated to pursue Petty Trade. As this trade is highly sensitive to location and its local demand which can saturate at any time, many beneficiaries undertaking it had failed. This Study listed the main reasons for the poor performance of the beneficiaries under Industries Department as follows: (i) lack of adequate skills and experience on trade related activities, (ii) unavailability of enough working space, and (iii) limited option available to beneficiaries in the selection of their trades in view of their skills, experience, and interest.

8.4. Critical Gaps in Project Implementation

8.4.1. Mismatch between Physical Targets and Achievements

Physical targets for all sectors were made clearly at the preparatory stage of the project keeping in view the various natural factors like the potential lands for WRC, horticultural and plantation crops, fisheries, etc. Similarly, care was taken in setting physical targets for industrial activities and services sector, and the number was determined so as to meet existing demand for the products, especially of local demand. These targets were set to ensure balanced development across the different sectors using various research inputs and in consultation with experts of various fields. It was expected that attempt be made to ensure physical achievement according to these targeted pattern of distribution of beneficiaries among the different sectors. Table 8.4 presents the physical targets and achievement among the eight economic sectors under NLUP. As the activities under UD&PA were industrial trades in nature, they are clubbed together under Industries Department. Similarly, the physical targets of the original DPR also anticipated the existence of a considerable number of beneficiaries who could not be easily put under any one sector. Such targeted beneficiaries were put under industries as they are mostly accommodated under SME of Industries Department.

Table 8.4
Comparison of Sector-Wise Physical Targets and Achievement under NLUP

Sl. No.	*Sectors*	*Physical Target (No)*	*Physical Achievement (No)*	*Achievement Ratio (%)*	*Shortfall/ Surplus (%)*
1.	Agriculture	31600	19911	63.01	-36.99
2.	Horticulture	28800	23813	82.68	-17.32
3.	Soil & Water Conservation	8400	11854	141.12	+41.12
4.	Sericulture	8500	2206	25.95	-74.05
5.	Fisheries	3000	3654	121.80	+21.80
6.	Environment & Forest	10740	3282	30.56	-69.44
7.	Animal Husbandry & Veterinary	18860	37054	196.47	+96.47
8.	Industries	10100	30270	299.70	+199.70
	Total	**120000**	**132044**	**110.04**	**10.04**

Source: (i) *Detailed Project Report of NLUP,* Government of Mizoram, 2009; and (ii) *NLUP Implementing Board, Government of Mizoram,* Dated 29.05.2014.

Table 8.4 shows significant deviation of the physical achievements from the targeted number across the sectors. We may call it 'structural failure of physical achievement'. It is certain that this could be the main source of failure for the policy in the future, in addition to the management problems in its implementation. The two key land-based sector of agriculture and horticulture that the policy makers gave priority to recorded a shortfall of 36.99 per cent and 17.32 per cent respectively from their physical targets. Similarly, sericulture and environment and forest also recorded a shortfall of 74.05 per cent and 69.44 per cent respectively. Excepting Soil and Water Conservation and Fisheries departments, all land based sectors, where the government anticipated making a big push, achieved significantly lower than targeted number of beneficiaries.

The shortfall of physical achievement under key land based sectors were accounted for by excessively higher achievement ratio of Industries Department and AH & Vety Department. The two departments recorded a surplus of 199.70 per cent and 96.47 per cent respectively. The highly inflated number of beneficiaries under Industries Department was a result of the inclusion of urban areas under the scheme, where jhum cultivation is not practically in operation and enough space is not available for land based activities. The very notion of 'Land Use' was impracticable in most of the cases in urban areas, especially in Aizawl city. Similarly, the reason for the significantly higher physical achievement under AH & Vety Department would be the possibility that these trades could be easily implemented without proper skill and working space, while the assistance amounts are similar to other land based trades. As there was no inbuilt mechanism in the project guidelines to check major deviation of physical achievements from the desired targets for balanced progress of various economic sectors, there was a tendency among the selected beneficiaries to choose trades that they found were not demanding of skills, working space, and infrastructures, but carried similar amount of assistance, thus neglecting its scope of success. It becomes something like making easy money. It includes trades like petty trades, piggery, poultry, auto-rickshaw, hill cattle, etc. It is unfortunate that the government did not make any attempt worth mention to monitor the pattern of trade selection/allocation among the beneficiaries. The poor performance of the urban beneficiaries is clearly the result of this situation.

Given the existing staff position of the line departments, the total physical target of 1.2 lakh beneficiaries might have been too large for efficient management of the project implementation through input supplies, monitoring and evaluation, and capacity development. To add to this, the physical achievement was more than 10 per cent of the target. In fact, having higher physical achievement is desired on the ground that a large number of families who are poor and in need would be covered by the scheme. However, the problem that comes to the fore is its management. It is practically impossible to conduct regular monitoring, training, and switch action on input supply by the executing agency of the project due to the enormity of the number of beneficiaries *vis-a-vis* insufficient number of staff and their level of efficiencies. In addition, instead of sticking to the principle of need based allocation of the number of beneficiaries in each village, the authority allotted the number of beneficiaries in the villages more or less arbitrarily. This opened up space for the local political leaders to manipulate beneficiary selection to achieve their political interests.

8.4.2. Beneficiary Assistance versus Infrastructure Development

The NLUP project as approved by Cabinet Committee on Economic Affairs (CCEA), Government of India, envisaged three components of funding — management, infrastructure, and development components. Their original fund allotments were 2.51 per cent, 41.10 per cent, and 56.30 per cent respectively. Detailed annual financial allotment to these components showed excessively higher amount for development component (i.e. it ranged from 84.64 per cent to 93.59 per cent), while the percentage share for infrastructure component was less than 10 per cent across the years. Expenditure under the head of development component was primarily meant for beneficiary assistance in the form of cash and materials. As expenditure on infrastructure development was to be made through Convergence Scheme, these annual allocations were to be in the form of matching share contribution for converging CSS. The financial achievement for infrastructure development under Convergence Scheme is very low till date. This means that the NLUP has not contributed much towards infrastructure development in the state, over and above the normal trend of asset creation through CSS.

It is, thus, clear that NLUP is basically meant for direct beneficiary assistance, rather than indirect push through the provision of infrastructure development. Thus, the scheme can be considered *Beneficiary Approach* as the project intended to uplift the poor and shifting cultivators through delivery of direct assistance. The state government had in the past made several attempts, like NLUP, Jhum control, etc. to settle jhumia families in sustainable livelihood through the provision of direct assistances. Several researches in the past have observed that such kind of assistance had not been effective due to poor mechanism of delivery and monitoring on the part of the government departments, while the beneficiaries could not be held accountable to the purpose of the assistances and tended to divert the money to other purposes. In addition, the total number of beneficiaries covered by the scheme was too large for efficient management and monitoring, given the existing staff strength of the government departments. Thus, it is very likely that a large number of beneficiaries would divert their assistance for other family consumption needs. This sowed the seed for failure of the programme as a whole.

The main activity undertaken under NLUP scheme was distribution of beneficiary assistances. Initiative for infrastructure development lagged far behind, and even the media and general public did not give proper attention to it. Coordinated effort is necessary to achieve self-sufficiency in regular input supply for various agriculture and allied activities. It may be noted that the state is heavily dependent on other states (or neighbouring country of Myanmar) for the supply of inputs like fingerlings (fish), piglets, chicks, seeds of horticulture crops, etc., and the demand will further multiply in the future with the development of various agriculture and allied sector. So, in addition to providing one-time assistance to the beneficiaries, infrastructure development should be a thrust area for any attempt to attain sustainable agriculture development.

In fact, substantial amount was invested through the departmental ventures for improvement of input supply. Looking at the management failure of the government department in various government undertakings meant for production in the past, the sustainability of these infrastructures is highly questionable given the existing work culture among the department staff. An in-depth study on the demand-supply gaps of agriculture inputs and sources of inefficiency in operation and maintenance (O&M) of any venture under state government is necessary to chalk out effective policy interventions for infrastructure development. It may be more appropriate and dependable to facilitate private investment on input supply for agriculture and allied sector, rather than direct public investment that is subjected by O & M inefficiency.

The enormity of construction of agriculture link roads, as an activity for infrastructure development under NLUP, calls for further examination. As per the record of NIB, the total length of agriculture link road constructed till 2016 was 260 km long with a total expenditure of Rs. 13 crore. As no separate provision was made for the regular maintenance of these potential area link roads, their usability for the target farmers may be very low especially during the monsoon season. As even the roads under regular watch of the state Public Works Department are in a poor state due to heavy monsoon rains, the condition of un-surfaced link roads with no one responsible for its maintenance would be very poor. Effort is necessary from the government for regular maintenance of the assets and infrastructures developed under NLUP to leverage their potential impacts on the agriculture development.

Another area of concern is lack of reliable marketing policy. So far, the effort shown by the state government under NLUP towards development of marketing infrastructures for agriculture produce has only been the creation of physical assets like market sheds, godowns, storages, etc. The policy oversight includes lack of institutional reforms for agricultural marketing in Mizoram. No separate marketing laws or regulations has come up in sync, and the only rules in effect are the one being implemented through Trade and Commerce Department which were found to be inefficient and outdated to facilitate the coming of more quantity of market arrivals following NLUP. Notably, one effective institutional infrastructure under Agriculture Department is the enactment of 'Mizoram Oil Palm (Regulation of Production and Processing) Act, 2004'. This Act facilitates 'Contract Farming' for oil palm cultivation in Mizoram, which is also one of the adopted trades under NLUP. Emergence of such kinds of agricultural marketing regulations meant for marketing of various crops side by side with the development of physical infrastructures is necessary.

To sum up, to achieve sustainable agriculture development through government intervention schemes like NLUP, it is necessary to have synchronous efforts on development of beneficiaries through efficient delivery of assistance, infrastructure development, and development of physical and institutional infrastructure for agriculture marketing. Of the three areas, NLUP has given strong impetus on beneficiary assistance, while showing relatively poor (or negligible in some cases) and fragmented efforts on infrastructure development and marketing policy.

8.4.3. Land Resource Management

Proper land use planning and land management should be the starting point of any land-based policy, and NLUP is no exception. The policy guidelines clearly set out sustainable land use targets to be achieved by the project. It envisioned around 60 per cent of the total geographical areas to be dense forest, 10 per cent for catchment area forest, 10 per cent for community supply reserve, 15 per cent for land based NLUP activities, and five per cent for human settlement and developmental activities. Moreover, the policy's desired goal to achieve sustainable land use practices was to be implemented through three main approaches. They are: (i) one village–one crop; (ii) compact area approach; and (iii) cluster approach. In respect of land allotment and distribution, the Village Councils were authorised to allot land to the NLUP beneficiaries to undertake their trades. However, permanent allotment of land and issue of land pass was to be done by Department of Land Revenue and Settlement (DL and S). An NLUP beneficiary who had successfully utilised the land for the purpose it was allocated would be issued Land Settlement Certificate (LSC) by DL and S.

Although all the proposed land resource management practices under NLUP were appreciated, the reality was significantly different from its desired goal. There was no effective mechanism to monitor land allotment and its further utilisation. Sustainable land use practices mentioned above were hardly found in any place, thus posing serious problems for further policy intervention and building of infrastructure like link roads. A more distressing situation is lack of coordination between the NLUP activities and land assessment undertaken by DL and S. Consequently, most of the land freshly allocated for NLUP beneficiaries are yet to be assessed and surveyed for issue of LSC. Thus, these beneficiaries are not given legal entitlement for the land in which they cultivate their crops. The revenue Rules enacted post-NLUP in 2013 did not make any special mention about land allotted for NLUP activities. This shows the absence of coordinated efforts among the government departments for the successful implementation of the flagship programme of the government.

8.4.4. Unequal Participation of Stakeholders for Project Management

The project adopted an attractively decentralised model by introducing four-tier management system — Apex Board and NIB at the state level, District Level Implementing Committee (DLIC), and Village Level Implementing Committee (VLIC); while the line departments took the responsibility of all the ground works. In addition, there are monitoring committees at the state level, district level, and village level under NIB, DLIC, and VLIC respectively. It would have been the most successful and emulative management practice had the system worked properly. However, actual implementation of the scheme did not show efficient functioning of these stakeholders. While the active participation of the village level institution is key to the success in project management and monitoring, the role they played was limited to the selection of beneficiaries only. According to the study by CCN in 2015, the village level committee unexpectedly disappeared from the scene of monitoring of the performance of the beneficiaries. Even the villagers did not know the members of NLUP implementing and monitoring committees in their villages. This is, according to the opinion of knowledgeable persons interviewed, mostly due to politicised appointment of members of the ruling party as members of the VLIC, which made the people confused about whom, in effect, were the members of such committees.

The poor performance of the monitoring committees at various levels to monitor and evaluate the performance of the beneficiaries and other stakeholders is another critical area. As can be seen in Table 8.3, almost half of the beneficiaries of industrial sector did not take any initiative towards their trade, but were given the subsequent instalments of their assistances. As per the policy guidelines, those who did not take initiative on their trade were not to be given the next instalment. Since the case of industrial sector is considered a representing one for all other sectors especially for the performance of monitoring mechanism, it is clear that there was no effective monitoring system which had direct linkage with other stakeholders of the policy. A senior staff in one line department who claimed anonymity stated that the monitoring mechanism could not be effective as expected because of the frequent interferences and overruling of the decision made by field staff from the higher authority. Beneficiaries found not working were frequently recommended to the higher authority by the field staff to stop their further assistances. On knowing that, the beneficiaries sought help from their political boss so that their assistance can be continued, on which the latter took immediate action in their support. If this is the case, it may be a herculean task to ensure the existence of strict monitoring system in the implementation of the scheme.

8.5. The Way Forward

The state government had implemented NLUP three times in Mizoram to abolish jhum cultivation and uplift the poor families by providing sustainable means of livelihood. The main difference of NLUP 2011 from its predecessors is that it is comprehensive in nature and encompasses a wide range of activities for beneficiary assistance, infrastructure development, and marketing policy. Although there are several areas where the programme has not been successful as expected, this study observed visible decline in jhum area and significant changes in the scenario of agriculture and allied sector post-project. The livelihood conditions of a large number of families in rural and urban areas have been changed by this project. Further, the strong commitment of the political leaders who are in the ministry for its success is also commendable. Having implemented such a massive public programme with widespread involvement of various stakeholders in its implementation, it is time for the government to re-introspect, learn from its mistakes, and show efforts to sustain its positive impact for the development of the state. Based on the analysis reported in this book, the following points may be raised to enhance the success of this scheme and effectiveness of subsequent policy interventions in the future.

Firstly, the starting point for the successful implementation of any land use policy should be proper land use planning and its sustenance. The NLUP 2011 proposed desired land use practices like *cluster approach*, *one crop-one village*, and *compact area approach*. These approaches are desirable, and have the potential to improve the viability and effectiveness of further policy interventions in the future. However, they were not achieved due to a number of reasons like the haste of the public as well as political leaders for the commencement of the scheme, absence of proper mechanism to monitor and mobilise the stakeholders towards these goals, the enormity of the scheme in terms of targeted families, lack of public awareness on the expected benefits, etc. Future land use projects may not be initiated in the state without having a clear set of strategies and approaches for sustainable land use practices as it could disturb the existing system of cultivation rather than improve it. Moreover, it is necessary to evolve institutional reforms in land tenure system to prevent the emergence of unwanted land relations in the future, which can result from intervention in the existing system of land utilisation.

Secondly, it is necessary to change the perception of the academicians as well as the government towards jhum cultivation. Jhumming should not simply be considered as the worst form of cultivation, but be accepted as a part of tribal culture and living to which the people have strong attachment. Instead of attempting to abandon it through a strong policy push all of a sudden, there should be gradual shift of the people from jhumming to other means of livelihood. This is what most land use projects in the past have failed to consider.

Thirdly, the existence of proper marketing policy is one of the keys to the success of any project that strives to push production of agriculture and allied crops. Although NLUP has envisaged a set of marketing policies, the only visible efforts shown were building of physical infrastructures at different places without proper basis for the identification of strategic market location. A successful agricultural marketing policy should introduce institutional reform to facilitate the emergence of organised marketing system and the growth of the existing institution in a sustainable way.

Fourthly, as the state had implemented different schemes for the development of agriculture sector mostly by following *beneficiary approach* (i.e. giving assistance to farmers), we have also seen many drawbacks in their implementation. It may be more effective to evolve government policy towards infrastructure development in agriculture sector, which aims at self-sufficiency in input supply, link road, productivity improvement, marketing and storage infrastructures, quality control, etc. However, government intervention should be restricted to the areas where markets fail (i.e. where private sector are unlikely to invest in it), and the ventures in which the existing managerial-entrepreneurial capacity of the government agency is competent enough to efficiently undertake the day to day requirements of the operation and management.

Fifthly, the NLUP created well structured management framework for its implementation with a scope of grassroots stakeholders in the implementation and decision making. As noted earlier, the role played by grassroots institutions (e.g. village level monitoring committee) was very low. Such a massive policy directly affecting more than half of the population of the state requires people's participation at all levels of its implementation, and their limited participation can lead to a major failure. Given the efficiency levels and capacity of the government departments, it is advisable that major polices like NLUP may not be implemented in haste with only a span of five years. It should rather be in a phased manner spanning a longer term so as to give enough time for preparation and to ensure effective project management.

Lastly, the introduction of 'convergence scheme' under NLUP is commendable and worth emulating. The success of this scheme could prevent duplication of work and pull funds received from various sources together in order to execute works that are required to achieve agriculture development. This is more relevant in the area of infrastructure development. Convergence of activities is necessary not only in agriculture and allied sector, but also in all other developmental activities of the state. To achieve well-functioning system for convergence of various developmental works, it may be necessary to constitute steering committees or joint coordination committees of various departments, to identify works that can be brought under one scheme and to coordinate the execution of works.

REFERENCES

1. Clarke, Julian (1980), 'Peasantisation and Landholding' in Klein, Martin A. (Ed) *Peasants in Africa,* Sage Publication, London.
2. Conklin, H.C (1961), 'The Study of Shifting Cultivation', *Current Anthropology,* 2(1).
3. Consultative Committee for NLUP (2015), *A Study on the Success and Impact of NLUP under Horticulture Sector in Mizoram: Mandarin Orange,* NLUP Implementing Board, Government of Mizoram.
4. Das, Kalpana (2004), *Rural Development in Mizoram — A study of IRDP,* Mittal Publication, New Delhi.
5. Directorate of Census Operation, *Primary Abstract of Population Census, 2011,* Mizoram.
6. Garbyal, S.S (1999), 'Jhumming (Shifting Cultivation) in Mizoram (India) and New Land Use Policy — How far it has succeeded in containing this primitive agriculture practice,' *Indian Forester,* Vol. 125, Issue No. 2 (Feb), pp.137-148.
7. Government of Mizoram, *Basic Statistics (Various Issues),* Directorate of Economics and Statistics.
8. Government of Mizoram, *Draft Annual Plan for New Land Use Policy 2013-14.*
9. Government of Mizoram, *Economic Survey of Mizoram (Various Issues),* Department of Planning and Programme Implementation.
10. Government of Mizoram (2014), *The Mizoram (Land Revenue) Rules 2013,* Directorate of Land Revenue & Settlement, Linkman Publications, Kolkata.
11. Government of Mizoram, *Revised Guidelines on Mizoram Intodelhna Programme (MIP),* Notifications No.G.28014/11/2004-AGR, the 16 May 2006.
12. Government of Mizoram (2009), *Comprehensive Project under New Land Use Policy for Sustained Economic Development and the Uplift of the Poor in Mizoram.* Detailed Project Report submitted to the Planning Commission, NLUP Implementing Board.
13. Government of Mizoram (2009), *New Land Use Policy Manual,* NLUP Implementing Board.

14. JICA (2014), *The Study on Development and Management of Land and Land and Water Resources for Sustainable Agriculture in Mizoram,* Nippon Koei Co., Ltd., Tokyo, Japan.
15. Lawma, T (1991), *Perspective Plan for Conservation, Management and Development of Land Resources in North-Eastern Region of India,* unpublished project report, North Eastern Hill University, Shillong.
16. Lalchungnunga, K (1990), *A Mizo Village: Its Socio-economic-culture-relations and administrative aspects,* Unpublished Ph.D Thesis, Gauhati University.
17. Lalthangliana, B (1980), *History of Mizo in Burma,* MA Dissertation, Mandalay University.
18. Lalnunmawia, F, Tawngenga, Gopichand, P, and Lalriliana, F (2016), 'Emerging Land Use in Mizoram and Research Priorities' in Karlyn Eckman and Laltanpuii Ralte (Edited) *Integrated Land Use Management in the Eastern Himalayas, Vol. 2, Focus on Mizoram,* Akansha Publishing House, New Delhi.
19. Leblhuber, ShahnazKimi and Vanlalhruaia, H (2012), 'Jhum Cultivation versus the New Land Use Policy: Agrarian Change and Transformation in Mizoram.' In *Fields and Forests: Ethnographic Perspectives on Environmental Globalization,* Daniel Munster (Ed), Rachel Carson Center Perspectives, No. 5, pp.83-89.
20. Lianzela (1997), 'Effect of Shifting Cultivation on the Environment with Special Reference to Mizoram', *International Journal of Social Economics,* Vol. 24.
21. Lianzela (2008), 'Political Economy of Mizoram: A Study of MIP', *Mizoram Dimensions and Perspective,* Jagadish K. Patnaik (Edited), Concept Publishing Company Pvt. Ltd, New Delhi, pp.140-152.
22. Maithani, B.P (2005), *Shifting Cultivation in North-East India: Policy Issues and Options,* Mittal Publication, New Delhi.
23. Majumdhar, D.N. (1990), *Shifting Cultivation in North East India,* (Edited) Omsons Publication, Guwahati.
24. Menon, Ramesh (1988), 'Mizoram Makes Official Plan to Stop Shifting Cultivation', *India Today,* January 15, 1988.
25. Ministry of Statistics and Programme Implementation (2013), *Household Ownerships and Operational Holdings in India,* Report of the NSS 70th Round, Government of India
26. Mishra, V.K and Saha, R (2007), 'Characterisation of soil health under different land use pattern in hilly eco-system of Meghalaya', *Envis Bulletin* 15 (1&2).
27. Mizoram University (2015), *Survey and Impact Analysis of NLUP Beneficiaries under Industries Sector in Mizoram,* Department of Economics.
28. NABARD Consultancy services (2013), *Mid Term Assessment Report on New Land Use Policy of Government of Mizoram,* NABCONS Ltd., Mumbai.
29. Ralte, Laltanpuii (2015), 'Sustainable Agriculture Development in Mizoram,' *International Journal in Management and Social Science,* Vol. 3, No. 8 (August), pp.10-27.
30. Ralte, Laltanpuii (2016), 'An Introduction to Mizoram' in Karlyn Eckman

and Laltanpuii Ralte (Edited) *Integrated Land Use Management in the Eastern Himalayas, Vol. 2, Focus on Mizoram,* Akansha Publishing House, New Delhi.
31. Ray, A.C. (1982), *Mizoram Dynamics of Change,* Pearl Publishers, Kolkata.
32. Sati, V.P. and Rinawma, P (2014), 'Practices of Shifting Cultivation and Its Implication in Mizoram, North East India: A Review of Existing Research,' *Nature and Environment,* Vol. 19(2), pp.179-187.
33. Seletthanga (1990), *Pipu Lenlai,* Lianchhungi Book Stall, Aizawl.
34. Shakespeare, J (1917), *The Lushai Kuki Clans,* Macmillan & Co. Ltd. London.
35. Shimray, U.A. (2008), 'Land Use System in Manipur Hills: A Case Study of the Tangkhul Naga,' in Fernandes, Walter and Barbora, Sanajay (Edited) *Land, People and Politics: Contest Over Tribal Land in North East India,* North Eastern Social Research Centre, Guwahati.
36. Singh, Daman (1996), *The Last Frontier People and Forest in Mizoram,* Tata Energy Institute, New Delhi.
37. Singh, Daman (2007), 'The New Land Use Policy: People and Forest in Mizoram,' *Environmental Issues in India: A Reader,* Mahesh Rangarajan (Ed), Pearson Education (Kindle Book).
38. Sinha, Harendra (2012), *Bureaucracy and Rural Development in Mizoram,* Concept Publishing Company Pvt. Ltd., New Delhi.
39. Thangchungnunga (1993), *The Problem of Land Utilisation and The Place of Land Resources in the Economic Life of the Mizo Society,* Unpublished Ph.D Thesis, Gauhati University.
40. Thangchungnunga (1997), 'Shifting Cultivation and Emerging Pattern of Change in Land Relation,' *Naturral Resource Management in Mizoram Vol. I,* L.K. Jha (Edited), APH Publication, New Delhi.
41. Upadhyaya, K.K and Jha, L.K (1997), 'Role of Tenancy in Deforestation and Some Measures for its Control,' *Natural Resource Management in Mizoram Vol. 1,* L.K. Jha (Ed), APH Publication, New Delhi.
42. Zoramchhana, R (2000), *New Land Use Policy and Rural Development in Mizoram,* Unpublished M.Phil Dissertation, Department of Geography, North Eastern Hill University, Shillong.

APPENDIX

Table A1: District Wise Number of NLUP Beneficiaries in Mizoram

Department/Sector	*Mamit*	*Kolasib*	*Aizawl*	*Champhai*	*Serchhip*	*Lunglei*	*Lawngtlai*	*Saiha*	*Total*
Agriculture	1967	1791	3090	3273	2107	3698	3665	599	20190
Horticulture	3527	1970	3603	3136	2822	4777	2687	1346	23868
S & WC	912	2672	2868	702	690	2462	805	342	11453
Sericulture	117	193	755	328	208	365	63	165	2194
Fisheries	606	537	439	489	279	523	592	164	3629
E & F	162	131	432	614	230	1382	329	2	3282
AH & Vety	2848	2505	11629	6517	1587	4797	3997	3162	37042
Industries	1147	1577	13892	2325	1553	4029	1759	860	27142
UD & PA	—	—	3271	—	—	—	—	—	3271
Total	**11286**	**11376**	**39979**	**17384**	**9476**	**22033**	**13897**	**6640**	**132071**

Source: NLUP Implementing Board, Govt. of Mizoram, Dated 5th October, 2016

S & WC : Soil & Water Conservation

E & F : Environment and Forest

AH & Vety : Animal Husbandry & Veterinary

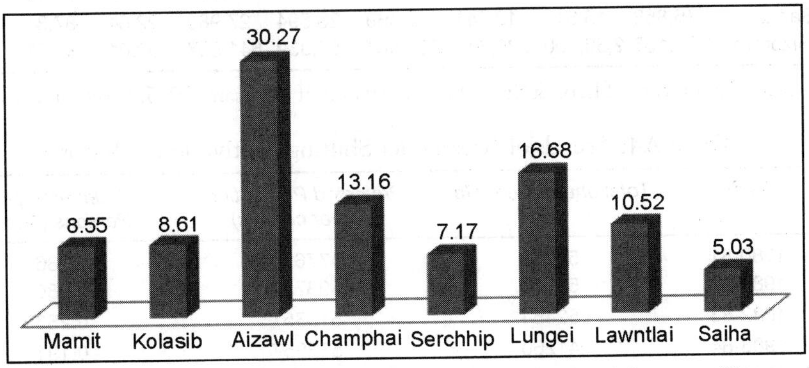

Fig.: District Wise Distribution of NLUP Beneficiaries in Mizoram (Percent)

Table A2: Basic Indicators of Population of Mizoram as per Decadal Census

Year	Population (No. of Persons)			Literacy Rate (%)			Density per Sq Km
	Male	Female	Total	Male	Female	Total	
1901	39,004	43,430	82,434	–	–	–	–
1911	43,028	48,176	91,204	–	–	–	–
1921	46,652	51,754	98,406	–	–	–	–
1931	59,186	65,218	1,24,404	–	–	–	–
1941	73,855	78,931	1,52,786	–	–	–	–
1951	96,136	1,00,066	1,96,202	46.15	16.70	36.23	9
1961	1,32,465	1,33,598	2,66,063	53.40	34.70	44.00	13
1971	1,70,824	1,61,566	3,32,390	60.49	46.71	53.79	16
1981	2,57,239	2,36,518	4,93,757	79.36	68.61	74.26	23
1991	3,58,978	3,30,778	6,89,756	85.61	78.60	82.27	33
2001	4,59,109	4,29,464	8,88,573	90.71	86.75	88.80	42
2011	5,55,339	5,41,867	10,97,206	93.35	89.27	91.33	52

Source: Directorate of Economics & Statistics, *Basic Statistics of Mizoram, 2015*, Govt. of Mizoram

Table A3: District Wise Population Details in Mizoram as per Population Census 2011

District	Rural		Urban		Total		Literacy Rate (%)		
	Male	Female	Male	Female	Male	Female	Male	Female	Total
Mamit	37,135	34,330	7,693	7,206	44,828	41,536	89.13	80	84.93
Kolasib	19,097	17,980	23,821	23,057	42,918	41,037	94.57	92.38	93.50
Aizawl	43,780	41,775	1,55,490	159264	199,270	201,039	98.11	97.67	97.89
Champhai	39,110	38,106	24,278	24,251	63,388	62,357	97.21	94.59	95.90
Serchhip	16,643	16,275	16,208	15,811	32,851	32,086	98.28	97.53	97.91
Lunglei	47,577	45,099	35,314	33,438	82,891	78,537	92.04	85.49	88.86
Lawngtlai	49,940	47,124	10,659	10,171	60,599	57,295	74.12	57.12	65.88
Saiha	15,853	15,611	12,741	12,369	28,594	27,980	92.64	87.34	90.01
Mizoram	269,135	2,56,300	286,204	285,567	555,339	541,867	92.01	86.56	89.36

Source: Directorate of Eco. & Stats, Basic Statistics of Mizoram, 2015, Govt. of Mizoram.

Table A4: Trends of Area under Shifting Cultivation in Mizoram

Year	Total Jhum Area (Ha)	Projected Population (as per census)	Jhum area per Persons (Acre)
1980-81	55265	477620	0.286
1981-82	55858	493757	0.280
1982-83	52484	513357	0.253
1983-84	41260	532957	0.191
1984-85	43377	552557	0.194

Year	Total Jhum Area (Ha)	Projected Population (as per census)	Jhum area per Persons (Acre)
1985-86	45920	572157	0.198
1986-87	38892	591756	0.162
1987-88	37803	611356	0.153
1988-89	36616	630956	0.143
1989-90	38349	650556	0.146
1990-91	36716	670156	0.135
1991-92	39175	689756	0.140
1992-93	43858	709638	0.153
1993-94	43234	729519	0.146
1994-95	46854	749401	0.154
1995-96	45423	769283	0.146
1996-97	43652	789165	0.137
1997-98	46691	809046	0.143
1998-99	46634	828928	0.139
1999-00	36285	848810	0.106
2000-01	35798	868692	0.102
2001-02	40305	888573	0.112
2002-03	41356	909436	0.112
2003-04	43447	930300	0.115
2004-05	40969	951163	0.106
2005-06	40100	972026	0.102
2006-07	41465	992890	0.103
2007-08	44947	1013753	0.110
2008-09	40792	1034616	0.097
2009-10	36841	1055480	0.086
2010-11	28562	1076343	0.066
2011-12	25826	1097206	0.058
2012-13	24706	1118070	0.055
2013-14	23150	1138933	0.050
2014-15	20064	1159796	0.043
CAGR (%)	-1.50	2.60	-3.99

Source:

i) Directorate of Agriculture, Statistical Abstract, (Various issues), Government of Mizoram

ii) Planning & Progamme Implementation, Economic Survey (Various Issues), Government of Mizoram

Note: Population figures between the Census Years are projected using the average growth rate.

CAGR (%) = Compound Annual Growth Rate (in Percent)

Table A5: Land Use Statistics of Mizoram

In thousand hectares

Year	Geographical Area	Forest Area	Not available for cultivation		for other uncultivated Land excluding fallow Land			Fallow Land		Net Area Sown	Net Area Irrigated
			Land put to non-agricultural use	Barren and Inculturable Land	Permanent pasture and other grazing land	Land under miscelleneous tree crops and groves not included in net Area sown	Culturable Waste	Fallow Land other than current fallow land	Current fallow land		
2000-01	2108.700	1626.475	121.790	8.600	22.500	30.600	5.310	155.809	36.285	101.331	9.686
2001-02	2108.700	1626.475	122.690	7.800	22.500	19.163	5.100	163.382	35.798	117.812	10.219
2002-03	2108.700	1550.608	125.190	7.800	13.100	27.253	9.500	215.713	41.356	117.78	10.669
2003-04	2108.700	1593.500	125.010	8.920	5.650	15.123	5.950	194.378	38.447	121.722	11.352
2004-05	2108.700	1593.650	125.510	8.520	5.346	10.232	5.000	181.199	49.969	123.564	11.852
2005-06	2108.700	1593.700	125.410	8.620	5.340	10.238	5.231	197.192	40.969	122.000	11.800
2006-07	2108.700	1593.700	125.420	8.620	5.235	68.765	5.230	166.078	41.465	94.187	11.388
2007-08	2108.700	1593.700	125.430	8.620	5.230	66.749	5.230	165.981	44.947	92.813	9.446
2008-09	2108.700	1593.700	124.000	9.000	5.250	51.976	10.000	170.850	40.089	103.835	11.022
2009-10	2108.700	1585.305	86.712	8.250	5.250	38.710	6.700	180.800	66.023	130.226	10.244
2010-11	2108.700	1585.305	86.712	8.250	5.250	38.711	6.700	182.262	66.607	130.121	12.123
2011-12	2108.700	1585.305	86.794	8.250	5.250	40.868	6.700	183.115	61.188	131.230	12.700
2012-13	2108.700	1585.305	86.880	8.250	5.250	41.083	6.700	194.031	50.380	130.821	14.330
2013-14	2108.700	1585.305	91.280	8.250	5.250	73.362	6.700	161.132	47.073	130.049	15.620
2014-15	2108.100	1585.305	42.000	7.450	4.250	32.050	5.700	165.368	48.151	214.184	16.380

Source: Directorate of Economics & Statistics, Basic Statistics of Mizoram, 2015, Government of Mizoram.

Table A6: Area and Production of Major Agriculture and Horticulture Crops in Mizoram

A = *Area* & P = *Production*

Year	Paddy		Maize		Pulses		Oilseeds		Sugarcane		Potato		Orange			
	A (Ha)	P (MT)	A (Ha)	P (MT)	A (Ha)	P (MT)	A (Ha)	P (MT)	A (Ha)	P (MT)	A (Ha)	P (MT)	A (Ha)	P (MT)	A (Ha)	P (MT)
2005-06	56460	107740	11742	22703	6861	8663	5870	5560	1383	15953	953	3891	5258	33020	4520	104818
2006-07	52851	42091*	10775	20969	5054	5833	4075	3755	1340	12187	639	1652	5395	34366	5020	119676
2007-08	54541	15688	7328	729	5048	2632	8485	748	883	828	330	1158	6395	11567	6220	98800
2008-09	51990	68917	9558	9318	3931	3646	3275	2514	1342	13696	269	1569	8275	10757	7220	66424
2009-10	47204	66132	8551	11510	3920	6479	2741	2988	1434	12368	285	2235	5348	13265	8660	84810
2010-11	40692	67428	9005	13499	3957	6065	3140	3727	1418	7900	431	3699	6516	19700	10040	115360
2011-12	38976	75566	6905	8397	3836	5332	2474	2382	1463	7456	409	2868	8360	22230	10090	119060
2012-13	39342	77471	6172	8064	3099	3288	2963	2224	1323	6795	286	1440	8960	24100	10540	127534
2013-14	38803	58994**	5793	8221	3862	5657	2059	2370	1421	6979	352	2961	13508	40430	10840	140920
2014-15	36930	60679	5695	8624	4221	5971	2137	2397	1476	44257	207	1282	14200	41200	10870	141000

Year	Grapes		Cabbage		Passion fruit		Tomato		Birdeye Chilly		Chow Chow		Turmeric		Ginger	
	A (Ha)	P (MT)	A (Ha)	P (MT)	A (Ha)	P (MT)	A (Ha)	P (MT)	A (Ha)	P (MT)	A (Ha)	P (MT)	A (Ha)	P (MT)	A (Ha)	P (MT)
2005-06	107	1521	275	4287	929	3354	16	274	714	721	604	21593	522	9735	4654	45143
2006-07	276	4217	236	3684	1109	4979		225	792	1077	664	24455	535	10074	3426	55432
2007-08	672	10416	200	5000	8944	44720	17	298	100	200	714	26418	4175	83500	3587	57010
2008-09	1172	9962	2985	38805	4084	13530	620	4960	7185	24429	3200	48000	9625	39862	10391	34290
2009-10	1232	13736	2400	21600	3150	16411	635	5715	8700	47850	2250	34875	4500	22500	6200	31000
2010-11	1575	19609	2600	33462	1522	6220	675	6075	8815	48483	3500	56350	4780	23900	6500	32500
2011-12	1880	24300	2800	37100	450	900	700	6420	8900	9790	4000	66500	5580	29240	7010	34460
2012-13	2380	20801	3020	40080	700	1470	800	7390	9020	8208	4500	75020	6050	22990	7280	28390
2013-14	2450	23870	3230	43280	838	1940	880	8270	9040	9100	4660	80020	6250	24700	7480	29920
2014-15	2450	22550	3680	48810	980	2110	1070	10120	9140	9330	4800	81930	6350	24130	7650	31200

Source: Directorate of Economics & Statistics, *Basic Statistics of Mizoram, 2015*, Government of Mizoram.

* production of paddy has decreased sharply due to onset of Mautam famine (Bamboo flowering).

** since 2013-14, production and yield of paddy have been reported in terms of Rice.

Table A7: Sectoral Share of Gross State Domestic Product (At current Price)

Percent

No.	Sectors & Sub-Sectors	2004-2005	2005-2006	2006-2007	2007-2008	2008-2009	2009-2010	2010-2011
1	Agriculture	13.47	12.74	12.40	13.68	14.16	14.44	14.63
2	Forestry & Logging	8.90	8.03	7.48	6.76	5.92	5.55	4.72
3	Fishing	1.13	1.03	0.97	0.55	0.47	0.51	0.72
	Agriculture and Allied	**23.50**	**21.81**	**20.84**	**21.00**	**20.55**	**20.50**	**20.07**
4	Mining & Quarrying	0.30	0.21	0.33	0.44	0.53	0.32	0.28
a	**Sub-Total of Primary**	**23.80**	**22.01**	**21.17**	**21.44**	**21.08**	**20.82**	**20.35**
5	Manufacturing	1.40	1.31	1.45	1.57	1.31	1.15	1.09
5.1	Manu-Registered	0.21	0.28	0.18	0.18	0.12	0.13	0.18
5.2	Manu-Unregistered	1.19	1.04	1.28	1.39	1.19	1.02	0.91
6	Construction	10.78	14.36	13.68	13.65	16.08	15.01	12.63
7	Electricity, Gas and Water Supply	4.12	4.25	4.05	4.35	2.88	3.05	3.29
b	**Sub-Total of Secondary**	**16.30**	**19.92**	**19.19**	**19.57**	**20.27**	**19.21**	**17.01**
	Industry	**16.60**	**20.12**	**19.52**	**20.00**	**20.80**	**19.53**	**17.29**
8	**Transport, Storage & Communication**	**2.68**	**2.63**	**2.69**	**2.64**	**2.43**	**2.21**	**1.99**
8.1	Railways	0.01	0.01	0.01	0.01	0.01	0.01	0.01
8.2	Transport by other means	2.09	1.99	2.04	2.05	1.90	1.67	1.53
8.3	Storage	0.02	0.02	0.02	0.02	0.02	0.02	0.02
8.4	Communication	0.57	0.61	0.61	0.56	0.51	0.52	0.43
9	Trade, Hotels and Restaurants	9.59	9.71	10.02	10.25	9.94	9.83	9.16
10	Banking & Insurance	2.72	2.60	2.73	2.66	2.56	2.57	2.36
11	Real Estate, Ownership of Dwellings and Business Services	13.62	14.34	15.10	15.25	14.35	14.18	14.67
12	Public administration	18.46	16.72	16.68	15.78	16.75	18.52	20.84
13	Other Services	12.84	12.08	12.43	12.42	12.61	12.65	13.62
c	**Sub-Total of Tertiary**	**59.90**	**58.07**	**59.64**	**59.00**	**58.65**	**59.97**	**62.64**
14	State Domestic Product (Rs. lacs)	100.00	100.00	100.00	100.00	100.00	100.00	100.00
15	**Calculated State Domestic Product (Rs. lacs)**	**100.00**	**100.00**	**100.00**	**100.00**	**100.00**	**100.00**	**100.00**

Source: http://desmizo.nic.in/

INDEX